Courage, Compassion and Wisdom exist wonderful way of helping the reader see an interconnection of each of them. These are everyday people sharing Courage, Compas others – for the benefit of others, it takes a writer like Joan to help remind us all of the value of each of them.

    – Juliette White CBE, Senior Executive

The Three Companions offers a perspective of ourselves and how courage, compassion and wisdom can imbue our lives to allow us to thrive and be our best selves. The key here is to realise that each is already within us; recognising this reality changes everything. Powerful and profound.

    – James R. Doty, M.D., Founder and Director of the CCARE at Stanford University School of Medicine, and Senior Editor of the *Oxford Handbook of Compassion Science*

I enjoyed exploring the hypothesis that Courage, Compassion and Wisdom working hand in hand are essential to make the world a better place. A number of the examples were really inspirational and helped me reflect on my own personal journey. I found the analysis and practical guidance in the last section to be helpful in supporting one's personal journey of exploration.

    – Dapo Ajay, Senior Executive

I'm delighted by the way Joan has crafted an enlightening and practical guide that demystifies Courage, Compassion, and Wisdom. The engaging stories she has collected highlight the many facets of three human characteristics we all possess. I found her book to be both profound and enjoyable reading. I highly recommend *The Three Companions* for anyone looking to clarify their self-understanding and relationships with others.

    – Dan Newby, Founder of the School of Emotions and author of *The Unopened Gift: A Primer in Emotional Literacy* and *The Field Guide to Emotions*

THE
3
COMPANIONS

COURAGE, COMPASSION & WISDOM
the powerful keys to happier work
and a fulfilled life

Dr Joan van den Brink

For Jurgen, my beloved husband.
You brightened my life and augmented my world.

.

The Three Companions

ISBN 978-1-912300-60-0
eISBN 978-1-912300-61-7

Published in 2021 by SRA Books
Printed in the UK

Excerpt from 'Courage' printed with permission from Many Rivers Press, www.davidwhyte.com. David Whyte, *Consolations: The Solace, Nourishment and Underlying Meaning of Everyday Words*, © 2014, Many Rivers Press, Langley, WA USA.

Contents

Foreword by Nobantu Mpotulo   vii

Introduction   1

Part 1: Defining Courage, Compassion and Wisdom   **15**

Courage   19

Compassion   23

Wisdom   27

Working with the Three Companions   31

Finding an ideal way of being   33

Part 2: Displaying Courage, Compassion and Wisdom   **37**

Educating and developing yourself   41

Replenishing yourself   55

Coping with illness   65

The final moments of someone's life   89

Parenting   103

Handling strains in relationships   113

Helping others   125

Protecting and defending others   141

Dealing with crises   145

Resolving dilemmas with ethics and integrity   153

Challenging power   159

Leading people through change   177

Part 3: Developing Courage, Compassion and Wisdom   **187**

How to grow your Three Companions   191

Five domains to support the use of the Three Companions   199

In closing…   225

Notes   229

Acknowledgements   231

Foreword

I am thrilled and excited to be writing a foreword for this amazing book, *The Three Companions* by Joan van den Brink. The Three Companions are Compassion, Courage and Wisdom; this is what the world needs right now more than ever as we navigate the effects of the COVID-19 pandemic. The book shares very personal and everyday stories of ordinary human beings like me and you. I found *The Three Companions* to be a source of support and love for me personally, helping me take courageous acts of compassion when most needed. As a Buddhist teacher and practitioner, I found the book to be very practical as it introduces us to these wonderful concepts, shares the different *truths* of people who have demonstrated these gems and gives us practical tools and practices to develop these Three Companions. Compassion is different from empathy: empathy is an awareness and the ability to feel what another person feels, whereas compassion takes that further by taking action and doing something about another person's suffering.

I was struck by the coincidence and telepathy that occurred as I was reading the final pages of the manuscript. I got a message from LinkedIn from a stranger who had come across my bio and wanted to explore my personal and professional journey with me. As we were having this conversation, right at the beginning this person shared a personal experience of having lost her husband through suicide a few weeks beforehand. I was struck by how in the moment, with immediacy, I was called to exercise the Three Companions. As I was still reading the manuscript it was so easy for me to drop everything immediately and utilise them.

This well-timed book also talks to me on a cultural level as it links so well with the philosophy of *ubuntu*, an African wisdom which, when translated, means '*I am because we are*'. I cannot be fully me if you are not fully you. Nelson Mandela once said, 'In Africa there is a concept known as *ubuntu* – the profound sense that we are human only through the humanity of others; that if we are to accomplish anything in this world it will in equal measure be due to the work and achievement of others.'

If you are really moved to make a difference in the world this is the book for you. Enjoy the ride – thanks, Joan, for this gift to humanity.

Nobantu Mpotulo
Executive coach, leadership expert
Truth and reconciliation hearings facilitator

Introduction

I believe that courage, compassion and wisdom are three qualities that work hand in hand to enable us to approach difficult, emotive and sensitive situations in ways that empower the parties involved to have meaningful conversations. These dialogues lead to greater understanding of the situation, increased self-insights and eventually lasting change.

Using courage, compassion and wisdom – which I call the Three Companions – is both a skill and a way of being that is valuable in all aspects of our lives. They can be employed to tackle big issues such as inclusion, equity and belonging, mental health, the environment and sustainability, homelessness and much more. The Three Companions also equip us to handle smaller issues such as our day-to-day disappointments and upsets, and difficult conversations. In the workplace, there is an increased focus on inclusion (and diversity) and providing opportunities to level the playing field for disadvantaged groups. To be truly effective in tackling this complex issue, it is important to create the conditions in which people can speak up and share their experiences in the workplace without fear of judgement, ridicule or recrimination. Employing the Three Companions allows individuals to create a welcoming and safe space in which to have a discourse. They are able to truly see and hear each other and gain insights into those of their behaviours that lead to some people feeling hurt and excluded.

I am convinced that the Three Companions are essential qualities that we need to make the world a better place. These qualities are inherent in us all. However, I noticed that many of my friends and colleagues were unaware or denied that they possessed courage, compassion and wisdom. Yet my experience of them was that they epitomised these qualities, and I wanted to help them and others recognise the superpowers that they already possess and feel more confident in their ability to face challenging situations and solve complex problems.

I decided to write a book that showcased common examples of the Three Companions, so that people could see that they are present in ordinary situations and relate their own circumstances to the ones in the stories.

This book will help to equip individuals who are facing difficulties to anchor and centre themselves, put their situations into context and build their resilience. It is also a resource for anyone who wants to tackle delicate and emotive issues or handle dilemmas in a sensitive and caring way. The book covers personal and work situations because, as hard as we might try or pretend, we cannot enforce rigid boundaries between our work and private personas. What happens in our private lives impacts us at work and vice versa.

I believe this book will hold particular resonance for:

- Leaders who are passionate about people and want to create the conditions for them to thrive. It will help them to have meaningful conversations about complex people issues and consider ways to balance driving for performance with retaining a human approach.
- Chairs of employee resource groups, who need to advocate for their members to get the opportunities, support and resources they require to flourish in the workplace.[1]
- Chief Diversity Officers who are tasked with enabling inclusive environments and focused on best practices, providing thought leadership and development for all staff on diversity, equity and inclusion.
- Consultants and coaches who support individuals and organisations to be the best they can be.

- Individuals who are humanists and curious about how they can use courage, compassion and wisdom to greater effect.

You will get the most out of this book if you allow yourself to become involved in the content. Be open and curious. Ask yourself how you would handle similar situations: for example, in cases where you faced comparable circumstances, how did you behave? What did you feel? How did you act? Push yourself to find your own meaning in what is written here and elicit lessons that you can apply to your life.

Why courage, compassion and wisdom?

I am a Buddhist. In Buddhism, we identify courage, compassion and wisdom as the three virtues that allow us to alleviate suffering and achieve enlightenment. The Buddha, Shakyamuni, possessed these qualities. Courage, compassion and wisdom exist within us all and are manifest in myriad ways in our daily lives. However, we often associate physical acts of outstanding bravery with courage, and we tend to think of selfless human beings as those who perform amazing acts of humanitarianism or forgiveness, associating the likes of Malala Yousafzai, Desmond Tutu, Azim Khamisa[2, 3] with compassion and individuals such as the Dalai Lama and Nelson Mandela with wisdom. These are people we revere and look up to. For the most part, we connect the Three Companions with a select few who touch the lives of many. We tend to discount these qualities in ourselves.

In *The Wonderful Wizard of Oz* by L. Frank Baum, Dorothy's three companions are the Cowardly Lion, who desires courage, the Tin Man, who is seeking a heart (compassion) and the Scarecrow, who wants to have brains (wisdom). In the story, they accompany Dorothy to the Emerald City to obtain these qualities from the Wizard of Oz. What they discover is that they possessed these qualities all along.

Buddhism teaches us that courage, compassion and wisdom exist within us and are revealed under the right conditions. I have a friend who describes herself as timid and shy. However, when she spots an injustice, she is fearless in speaking out against it. That is a wonderful example of courage, compassion, and wisdom, which is not part of my friend's self-image. In this book, I want to help people access their true selves and discover their potency.

The power of living my purpose

The catalyst for this book came after I did some work in January 2020 to refine my own sense of purpose – why I get out of bed in the morning. Through that process I arrived at the statement: 'To create intimate environments so that people thrive.' This mission brings me energy and joy. I was considering how to live more wholly in accord with my purpose and, with gentle encouragement from my son, I started exploring the idea of writing a book. I doubted my ability to do this and my son's remark, 'Why not? You're a good writer', gave me both confidence and impetus. I realised that I needed to write about something that I knew a lot about and had a passion for. I alighted on the idea of writing about something that forms the bedrock of my life: courage, compassion and wisdom. This struck a deep chord within me. I coined the term 'the Three Companions' because I deeply believe in the power of these three qualities acting together in harmony. They empower us to have meaningful conversations about difficult and sensitive topics and to take action to alleviate suffering and create positive change. I feel this is particularly pertinent currently due to the tendency we have to hold binary views and the polarisation of opinions; for example, Brexit and Brin,[4] pro- and anti-vaccine, and right-wing versus left-wing politics. We need to have a more inclusive dialogue in which we seek to understand opposing views rather than close them down.

The journey then was for me to conduct some research to discover how the Three Companions manifest themselves in the lives of ordinary people and myself. I embarked on this exploration without knowing where it would end or the route I would take. All I knew was that I was answering an inner call that had previously been a whisper, but which I was now able to hear loud and clear. What was this plea? To use my talents in a better manner, to come out from hiding and touch the world in a more significant way. 'What does that mean?' you might ask. I had received feedback over the years about the positive impact I had on others and how something I said or did would often change their lives for the better. I didn't understand what I did, and still don't. All I knew was that I had a gift to help others and I wanted to figure out how I could harness this and be more intentional about inspiring others to be their best selves.

I had no idea of how to go about this and had positively shied away from writing a book in the past, so this was surprising and new territory for me. I tested my idea on a few people and was amazed and bowled over by the positive reception. I knew then I was on to something and set out in earnest on this project.

An important decision I made early in this process was to conduct interviews to hear the perspectives and stories of a diverse set of people. I wanted to be able to share these accounts in a way that revealed the different aspects and modes of courage, compassion and wisdom that are displayed in daily life. It was vital, to me, that I did not feature individuals whose job naturally required them to show the behaviours related to these values, such as firefighters, healthcare professionals, care workers and so on. If I wanted to help my readers access their own Three Companions, I needed to converse with people whom they could readily identify with.

The conversations that unfolded were deeply personal and humbling. I feel immense gratitude that these individuals willingly shared their thoughts and feelings and often brought up personal trials and tribulations that perhaps they would not normally discuss with others. The conversations were invariably enjoyable and enriching. I deepened my appreciation for the Three Companions and the nuanced and multi-faceted ways in which they can be expressed.

What I had not anticipated was the powerful impact that these conversations had both on me and the individuals I spoke with. This was apparent at the time and subsequently in later conversations I had with some of my interviewees. Each interview became a dialogue in a safe and trusting environment in which we listened to each other as we explored and shared our views and experiences on what it means to be courageous, compassionate and wise. I have been transformed by these conversations. I have opened my heart much more to my environment and the people in it. I now rely on my Three Companions much more in how I relate to others.

The backdrop

I started on my journey to write this book in January 2020, when the world still looked relatively normal. I saw 2020 as having the potential to be a pivotal year for me because I had plans to branch out in my work and devote my energies to living my purpose. I had contact with my regular clients and face-to-face workshops scheduled to occur throughout the year. Little did I realise then how dramatically the world would change for me and everyone else in eight short weeks! In addition to a personal bereavement in February, COVID-19 hit the world with force in March 2020 and life as we knew it changed overnight.

Fortunately, I was accustomed to working from home and already Zoom literate, so I was able to adjust to full-time remote working quite easily. I continued apace with my interviews for the book and, along with thousands of others, offered my services to several initiatives to provide *pro bono* coaching. It was clear to me that as the pandemic took hold and countries went into lockdown measures, my friends, family and colleagues needed to talk about their experiences of this crazy and scary new world. I strongly felt that now was a time when the Three Companions were needed more than ever. I established an online community, known as the CCW Community, for the people whom I had interviewed, to provide a safe space for them to have a different kind of conversation than they would have elsewhere. They could show up as they were and freely express their emotions and concerns, and connect with others. There was no need for them to put on a brave front or be strong. The Community was a place where they could express their anxieties and fears and think about their situations in terms of courage, compassion and wisdom. These groups took on a significance and meaning that I had not anticipated. I was thankful that group members were curious enough to join the meetings, and perceived sufficient benefit from them to keep returning more than a year later.

I thought that the CCW Community would run for three months, and after that we would get back to life as 'normal'. However, that was not the case. As the pandemic hit us with the force of a tornado, leaving a trail of destruction and devastation in its wake, people openly questioned the decisions of our political leaders, angered by the lack of clear and decisive leadership that could protect lives. There was a general undercurrent of anxiety that gave a tone and colour to all our discussions. Some felt this more acutely than others and it was always present even as we looked for things to encourage us and lift our spirits. This implies that we were down and/or depressed, and at times some of us were; however, the mood in the group was overwhelmingly positive and constructive. We had fruitful and interesting discussions that gave us ideas about how to navigate through this confusing time, increase our resilience and share our joys and laughter.

A tsunami of distress and dismay hit our shores with the killing of George Floyd by US police on 25 May 2020. We had some impassioned discussions in the CCW Community to process what his death signified to us. We saw the world tilt even further on its axis and took inspiration from the diversity of perspectives and experiences that enlightened us about the nature of racism and what we can do about it. Certainly, it is a time for our Three Companions to allow all voices to be heard.

This showed me that there was a continuing need to provide avenues for individuals to discuss these issues in ways that they had not done before or rarely got the opportunity to do. The CCW Community was serving an important purpose. I decided to continue hosting the group for long as there was someone who wanted to look at the issues of the day through that lens.

I learnt a lot through hosting this community. I discovered the power of connection and bonding that can form amongst strangers. I saw first-hand the value that an individual brings to a group solely by their presence and how this is further amplified by the nature of their contribution. This became poignant when regular group members were absent, and their presence was greatly missed by the other participants. I also realised that while a small proportion of the Community participated in the discussions, the wider group benefited from the weekly emails that I sent to share with them the themes that had emerged during that week's discussions (the groups met three times per week). I had a far greater impact on people than I realised!

The cast

I started the process of selecting interviewees for this book by contacting people I knew both to test whether my idea resonated with them and to get the ball rolling. I expanded my initial group by asking each interviewee to suggest other people whom I could speak to, and, through my own research, I reached out to individuals who had shown an interest in at least one of the qualities of the Three Companions through their own writing, research or other activities.

Through these conversations I met a diverse group of people, many of whom I did not know prior to embarking on the project. I interviewed a total of 65 people, 31 per cent of whom were male. Forty-two per cent of my interviewees were White British and another 20 per cent were White European, 15 per cent Black or Multi-racial, and 5 per cent Asian – Indian or Chinese. The majority lived in the UK, with a scattering of people in Africa, Australia, Europe, South East Asia and the USA.

The age profile was skewed towards individuals in their fifties and sixties, which is perhaps unsurprising given that I am sixty and I initially approached people within my network, most of whom are older in years, who in turn recommended their own peers in the main. However, I was also fortunate enough to talk to a few people in the younger age ranges

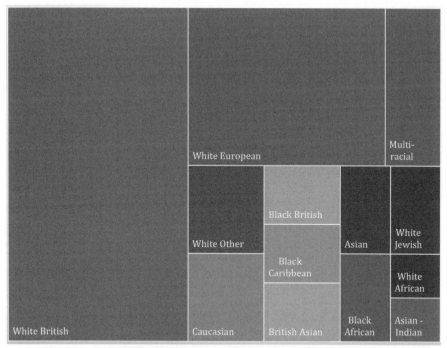

Figure 1: Ethnic profile of participants

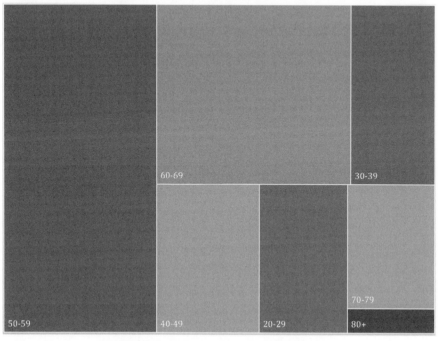

Figure 2: Age profile of participants

(twenties to forties), as well as those in their seventies and eighties. So, I feel I have covered the spectrum with the caveat that this is a biased sample based on a self-selecting group of interested people.

This book is based on their stories and there are, of course, many other voices still waiting to be heard.

The interview protocol

Before talking to my interviewees, I created a protocol that explained the purpose of the interview and which contained a pool of questions that I would draw from. I started the interview by gathering demographic data since I felt this would ease the interviewees into the conversation. I devised ten questions relating to the Three Companions. However, I am an organic person and like to go with the flow, so these questions were a guide for the conversation rather than a checklist. In fact, there were only two questions that I used consistently:

1. **When you hear the words courage, compassion, and wisdom, what do they mean to you?**
2. **Can you describe a time when you displayed courage, compassion and wisdom?**

I also used the question 'What would you like to see in the book?' to solicit information about the content the interviewees would find helpful. Many were interested in learning how to develop their Three Companions. That seemed like a natural place to go with this book; i.e., now that we have read people's stories, what are the implications for us?

I learnt early on that it was better to send the protocol in advance of the interview to allow the interviewee time to reflect on the content I was looking for. When we spoke, I started with a free-association with the words and allowed the conversation to flow from what emerged. I didn't feel it was necessary to cover all the questions in each interview, which resulted in a rich discourse in which we learnt from each other.

To make it easier for you to connect with their stories and to protect the identity of the interviewees, I have used fictitious names for them and the people they mention in these pages. I have also edited the text, with the approval of the interviewees, to convey the main points without diluting their voices.

Finding your way

As will become increasingly clear in the chapters that follow, I have a strong conviction that courage, compassion and wisdom together provide us with a way of being that is generous, nurturing and kind to ourselves and others. If we are truly open to what these qualities mean to us and how we can live our lives, we have the potential to grow and evolve as individuals and in so doing we will enable others to do the same. These values are about connection not isolation, about 'we' not 'I', about the individual and collective good, rather than individual gain. Very much the antithesis to how much of life is lived today.

The book is divided into three parts:

- Part One: Defining Courage, Compassion and Wisdom
- Part Two: Displaying Courage, Compassion and Wisdom
- Part Three: Developing Courage, Compassion and Wisdom

When I reviewed the accounts in the interviews, I was seeking what connected them: what were the circumstances in which individuals either chose or shied away from using the Three Companions? Some themes emerged, which led me to formulate practices that support us in using the Three Companions in our interactions with others. In Part One, we will therefore first explore what courage, compassion and wisdom mean to different people. I noticed that the stories could be organised into scenarios or themes and, in Part Two, I have arranged the stories according to the different types of situations that my interviewees faced. The accounts illustrate both those occasions when the storyteller displayed their Three Companions and those when they didn't, to allow us to learn from them.

Part Three describes a few practices that we can use to empower us by revealing and developing our Three Companions in ways that are meaningful to us personally. In it, I explain what each element is and offer some ideas about how to incorporate each component into your daily life. I then look at how the Three Companions act in concert and reinforce each other and how my interlocutors understood that connection.

A short parable

I mentioned earlier how my own practice of Buddhism has informed the approach in these pages. The Lotus Sutra is a religious text that is the foundation of many schools of Mahayana Buddhism. The 'Jewel in the Robe' parable — recounted in Chapter 8, 'Assurance for the Five Hundred Disciples', of the Lotus Sutra — is a wonderful illustration of the innate and hidden qualities that we possess to live an enriching life:

A poor man went to visit a rich man who was a good friend. They had a pleasant evening together, during which the wealthy friend plied his visitor with food and wine, and the man got drunk and fell asleep.

While the man was sleeping, his friend was called away on urgent business. However, the rich man first wanted to give his friend a priceless jewel as a gift. Not wanting to leave it lying around, he sewed it into the lining of the man's robe and left. After getting up, the poor man realised his friend was gone and went on his way. He travelled from place to place trying to find food and clothing, becoming more and more destitute.

Some years later, his friend happened to meet him and was shocked to see his impoverished state. He showed him the jewel that he had sewn into his robe all those years earlier. The poor man realised for the first time that he had a priceless jewel and was overjoyed.

There are many meanings that you can take from this parable, including the compassion of the rich man towards his friend. The one that relates to the innateness of the Three Companions is that the poor man had the means to transform his life but did not know this until his friend revealed it to him. I feel the same way about the Three Companions: we often don't know that we possess these qualities until the time is right for them to be revealed.

The time has come for you to discover your own precious jewels.

1

DEFINING COURAGE, COMPASSION AND WISDOM

When you hear the words 'courage', 'compassion' and 'wisdom', what do you think about? What do they mean to you?

As you read those questions, what happened? Did you try to answer them? Did you see them as rhetorical? What emotions arose as you read? However you regarded the questions, I invite you now to pause and truly reflect on what the words 'courage', 'compassion' and 'wisdom' evoke in you. What comes to mind? What somatic experience do you have? How do you feel?

When I interviewed people for this book, these were the first two questions I asked them about the Three Companions. I wanted them to free-associate with the words courage, compassion and wisdom. I wanted to know how people regarded them: what did they think about, how did they relate to them? I had no preconceived ideas of what I expected to hear and was accepting of what they had to say and curious to learn more. I explained my purpose in conducting the research and my interviewees decided whether they wanted to participate. They all saw the benefits of being more intentional about using the Three Companions. Many of them had not spent time thinking about what these words meant or how they applied to their lives. So the interview started an inquiry process for them.

These opening questions prompted answers that fell broadly into four groups:

- Aspirations and ideals to strive for.
- How these qualities impacted their way of being.
- Their interpretation of what each one meant.
- A visceral response to these words.

Reflect on your own free-associations – which group does your response fall within?

The responses that surprised me the most were the ones reporting a visceral reaction to the words. I knew that courage, compassion, and wisdom were 'big words', 'hard words' and ideals to live up to; I had never thought of the power of these words to physically affect people!

Jill described her reaction as: 'They make me stop in my tracks and they make me think.' This was amazing to me because I have only thought of the power of words to move me when they are written (and spoken) in poems or stories. I did not hear the music that came from these words alone. I did not experience the depth that is conveyed in these words until I embarked on the journey in this book and encountered remarkable people with different life experiences, viewpoints and ideas to share with me.

Regardless of which group their initial association fell into, most of the people I interviewed saw themselves as lacking at least one of the Three Companions. Most often this was wisdom, which many individuals associated with age. A few souls recognised that age is not synonymous with wisdom; children and many young adults display wisdom while those more mature in age may not. Wisdom is a way of being that is reflective of life's experiences and what we can learn from the accumulated experiences of others. The other Companion that often individuals felt they lacked was courage. This was partly due to how they defined it. Where interviewees saw courage as physical acts of bravery or heroism, they were less inclined to see themselves in that light.

Now that I have set the stage, let me give you some insights into how the people in my study defined the Three Companions and share what these qualities mean to me. You can see how your definitions relate to those that follow here.

Courage

I believe that courage is about deciding to do something that feels risky; you are unsure of success and there is some element of fear. This can range from 'small' things such as saying 'no' or expressing an opinion, to 'big' things like starting a new job, moving countries or having difficult conversations.

A personal example occurred many years ago and has stayed with me: it concerns an incident with my then-boss when I was in my thirties. He asked me to mask our poor performance to a major customer. I felt troubled by this. After reflecting, I decided to tell him I couldn't do it. My heart was pounding, and my voice was shaky as I told him. I was relieved when he said that was fine.

Individuals often conflate courage with an absence of fear; however, courage is about acting in the face of fear. There is an element of integrity and living up to personal values, despite the risk. Martina told me that she does this all the time, at a personal cost:

> Courage is about daring to be and do whatever is needed, even if that carries risk with it. For me, courage has been about speaking out about things that I perceive to be unjust, which often leaves me isolated or puts my head above the parapet or has me accused of being too serious or too intense or too something, all of that.

Two people introduced aspects of courage that I had not thought of previously. Camila associated courage with 'the decisive extrovert', people who 'step into the moment to deal with something'. She saw this strongly in others and less in herself. Rose, on the other hand, linked courage to resilience:

> You can't have courage without being resilient. I would define courage by saying something is in front of me that I have to face up to. It's something that I must move towards to deal with it. So that takes an internal strength and belief in myself that I am going to be able to deal with this.

I agree with this. Dr Taryn Marie Stejskal includes vulnerability and productive perseverance amongst her five practices of highly resilient people.[5] She also says that 'courage is the willingness to engage with fear.'[6]

What I learnt from a couple of my interviewees is that courage is also about doing inner work. It takes a lot to face aspects of ourselves that we do not like. Sabina described courage as tearing down inner walls:

> Courage is tearing those walls down within ourselves, or facing a change. I feel people might aspire to have a very stable life and courage really shows that people can let go of things and face the unknown, which is scary for many people.

Roger helped me to see a link between courage and compassion that had not occurred to me. To be alongside someone's suffering can trigger pain in ourselves; it takes courage to stay and be with them in our discomfort:

> Courage is what brings compassion into the world. If I feel the impulse to be there and to be engaged, I'm probably at the boundaries or beyond the boundaries of my comfort, so I sweat.

There is an interesting dimension to courage that is its relativity. Someone witnessing the act of another may regard this as being courageous by their own internal standards. However, the individual in question may or may not feel that they are being courageous. We can infer from this that what seems like a huge risk or challenge to one person could feel quite natural and ordinary to another. So how do we define courage? In the context of the Three Companions and acting intentionally, I think it is about how we feel rather than referring to an external standard.

I love David Whyte's thoughts on courage:

Courage

is a word that tempts us to think outwardly, to run bravely against opposing fire, to do something under besieging circumstance, and perhaps, above all, to be seen to do it in public, to show courage: to be celebrated in story, rewarded with medals, given the accolade. But a look at its linguistic origins is to look in a more interior direction and toward its original template, the old Norman French, *coeur*, or heart.

Courage is the measure of our heartfelt participation with life, with another, with a community, a work; a future. To be courageous is not necessarily to go anywhere or do anything, except to make conscious those things we already feel deeply and then to live through the unending vulnerabilities of those consequences. To be courageous is to seat our feelings deeply in the body and in the world: to live up to and into the necessities of relationships that often already exist, with things we find we already care deeply about: with a person, a future, a possibility in society, or with an unknown that begs us on – and always has begged us on. To be courageous is to stay close to the way we are made.[7]

Compassion

What does compassion mean to you?

If we look at the etymology of 'compassion', we see that it comes from the Latin root *pati*, which means 'to suffer', and *com*, which means 'with'. So, compassion literally means to suffer with. For me, there is an element of witnessing the suffering of another and being alongside them in that. Allowing them to be themselves without fear of judgement and to want that suffering to be alleviated.

Compassionate acts can vary greatly, including listening, acknowledging other people's feelings, performing acts of kindness, and showing we care. It is not about giving people unsolicited advice or taking responsibility for solving their issue. Sometimes, it is about giving tough messages; for example, if people are deluding themselves or in victim mode.

Buddhist compassion is the desire to relieve suffering and give joy. American Buddhist nun and spiritual teacher Pema Chödrön writes about compassion in *When Things Fall Apart*.[8] In Chapter 13, 'Widening the Circle of Compassion', she reminds us that to relate with others compassionately is challenging. She says that communicating to the heart and being there for others means not shutting down on them, which in turn means not shutting down on ourselves.

We reject in others what we reject in ourselves. Therefore, to be compassionate towards others, we need to be compassionate towards ourselves and accept every aspect of who we are. Pema Chödrön tells us that we can only see, hear and feel others as they really are when we create an open, non-judgemental space where we can acknowledge what we are feeling so that we are not caught up in that. When we do this, we can be with them. I aspire to be in this space with others. I think this is what interviewee Roger was referring to when he said, 'Courage is what brings compassion into the world.' This is hard!

Nathan felt that compassion was 'sublimating your ego and putting other people before yourself at the very core of it'.' My initial interpretation of this viewpoint was that in the moment that requires compassion, we recognise that it is about the other person and not ourselves. Reflecting on Pema Chödrön's words, I see that compassion is about ourselves and others equally.

Being with another compassionately is about respecting them as a human being and not fixing them. Javier articulated this when sharing his definition of compassion with me:

> **Sometimes you want to be understood. You want people to be kind. You don't necessarily want them to jump in and help. I do a lot of work with people who are working in the third sector, and you do meet some people who are just fixing machines. They want to jump in and fix everything for other people without trying to work out whether the kindest thing for that person is just to listen. A lot of people who are street homeless don't want your money. They want you to make eye contact. See them there as a person.**

Many interviewees linked empathy to compassion, the ability to step into someone's shoes and understand their experience and perspective. Grace made a thought-provoking observation that she could only show empathy if she had had a similar experience to the person in distress. In the absence of that, she was able to show compassion. Recently I have realised that it is incredibly difficult to show empathy. I find it hard to truly put myself in another's shoes. I have become humbler in not presuming I know how another feels. I think I mostly show compassion rather than empathy.

Also, I think there is a loving-kindness aspect to compassion. Loving-kindness is a traditional Buddhist concept that is about a concern for the happiness of others. Sabina put it eloquently:

> Compassion for me is love, which is not conditional. You can give it to anybody, and it's always there. I aspire to be a person who always has compassion because that's the answer to many things.

So do I!

Ava brought to my awareness the fact that compassion applies equally to animals as humans. I am not attached to animals, I don't have any pets, so this was a nuance I had not seen before. She told me:

> I think compassion, for me, is the root of kindness. It's the root of care. I don't believe that it's just a human quality because I think there are examples of animals behaving compassionately. And I think it's one of our traits that is very special, and there's a shortage of it.

Camila felt that 'compassion' as a word is overused. I was surprised by her view that it could be patronising. She felt there was an implied power imbalance in that the person acting compassionately is in a stronger place than the person in need. She felt uncomfortable with that. I believe that true compassion is being *with* another, so there is no feeling of superiority.

Roger posited that we can more reliably demonstrate compassion if we have a spiritual or reflective practice. I think this is true. The very essence of compassion is accepting our whole selves, including the parts we dislike. This takes a deep, personal enquiry.

There are many shades to compassion, as this discussion illustrates. At the heart of this, I believe that compassion is needed because human beings are flawed. At times we make mistakes, hurt ourselves and others, are thoughtless, have limited capabilities. We need compassion to accept that and make the most of the life that we have.

Wisdom

How do you relate to wisdom? Do you see yourself as wise? Is wisdom something you feel we are born with, or does it accumulate as we get older? Is wisdom only present in the elderly?

Personally, I think wisdom is about using our accumulated experience and learning to take the apposite action for the situation. This may be to do nothing. I believe wisdom leads to a positive outcome, which may be immediate or may take some time to be realised. For example, my daughter was heartbroken and felt abandoned by someone very close to her. I told her that, in time, she would forgive them, and the relationship would be restored. About three years later she told me, 'You were right that I would forgive them.' But this is not about me being right; the point here is that there can be distance between wisdom being dispensed and it being realised. Hugo captured my sentiments well:

Wisdom is a natural, authentic and relevant knowing that comes innately or which can be accessed due to pressure of circumstances. Part of it sits within the individual as inborn, and other parts are acquired through assimilation of lived experience.

Often, wisdom involves 'teaching moments' in which we share the knowledge and insights that we have gained. It can also be about supporting someone to make sense of their situation and what they want to change. Nathan put this succinctly:

Wisdom is the accumulation of knowledge and experiences, and the successful application of that learning to the challenges that life presents. With wisdom there's also an element of sharing.

I think to bring our wisdom to a situation we need to take the time to read what is occurring. What is happening? Why? What conclusions can we draw? What are the implications? What needs to happen next? This requires slowing down even for a few minutes. In today's world, we feel the pressure to have immediate answers, which makes it hard to access our wisdom.

Many of my interviewees felt that wisdom was something that elderly people had and that they themselves had not reached that state of sagacity. However, Martina explained that ageing had enabled her to be more at ease with who she is:

It's a bit of a cliché to say that wisdom comes with age, but I think it's true. I'm wiser now than I would have been in my twenties. And that's about understanding my place in the world. And much lighter, or much less fear around who I am in the world. I care less about what people think and things like that. So, all those kinds of things are about wisdom for me. Maturity as well.

I believe wisdom is innate, but we don't recognise this quality within us. Evie pondered this aspect of wisdom too because she experienced her children as having 'genuine, naive wisdom' in our technology-driven world. Milly, on the other hand, felt that age enables us to have a more holistic perspective on life and the limits of our knowledge:

I think wisdom is really to do with perspective. I think wisdom is a broad and long view. And understanding that what happens now isn't all there is. That's why I associate it with age. The longer the view, the better. And wisdom is an acceptance of the massiveness of your ignorance. I don't think you can be wise without understanding that it's a stab in the dark. You're trying your best to take the big view, but it's about maintaining openness to learn. Because you don't know most of what there is to know.

The point here is that we try our best to do the right thing, but we cannot know at the time if it is. Cameron shares a similar perspective. He has instilled in his children that they should make good choices, which are about future good for themselves or someone else. Lukas considered wisdom more broadly as being concerned with the greater good for all.

I suppose the level of wisdom that we possess is less contingent upon age and more dependent on our outlook on life. I surmise that we accrue wisdom throughout our lives, but we don't stop long enough to reflect on what we know. If we are open and curious, we will learn from dialogue, reading, witnessing others, in addition to our experiences. In this way, we can expand our levels of wisdom by accessing the collective wisdom of the universe and allow that to guide us. Amanda brought a spiritual dimension to this idea of shared knowledge:

I think children come into this world very wise. And we gain more earthly wisdom as we go through life. I believe we have greater wisdom because I think we've lived more than one life. So wisdom is about using that inner stuff.

Finn conceptualised wisdom in a different way to courage and compassion. He felt that he could see people who were courageous or compassionate. However, wisdom was more ephemeral and was something that he read about but couldn't grasp what it was. Matt had a similar admiration for individuals who seemed wise to him. He was left feeling, 'I wish I'd said that.'

If I could sum up wisdom, I'd suggest it's about slowing down enough to know the right thing to say or do in the moment.

Working with the Three Companions

We are used to thinking of courage, compassion and wisdom as standalone qualities, which, of course, they are. The power of the three of them working in concert allows us to operate from an optimal place where we are brave enough to start conversations that matter. We saw earlier that it is not easy to be alongside the suffering of another, to accept them as they are without judgement. In our compassion, we can feel their pain and it can be tempting to try to fix them rather than be with them. We need our wisdom to know how to show our compassion. What is needed? A quiet, healing presence? Honouring their dignity? Attention? Deep listening? Empathy? Advice? Fighting injustice?

One time that I called upon my Three Companions was when I decided to separate from my first husband, the father of my two children. His relationship with the three of us had broken down. I initially wanted to take the kids with me, but I realised that this would mean fighting him for custody. I didn't want that. Also, I travelled a lot for work at the time, so would have needed to get a live-in nanny. It didn't feel right to bring in a stranger to look after my children when they loved their dad and he wanted to rebuild his relationship with them. Instead, I decided to move out of the marital home and leave everything, to give them stability. I felt that I had the strength to retain the relationship with them and that has proved to be true. I have strong relationships with them both now, fourteen years later.

The intersection of courage, compassion and wisdom is a powerful place to be. The Three Companions go hand in hand. They modify each other so that courage does not become reckless and dangerous, compassion is not overwhelming, and wisdom doesn't morph into intellectual superiority. Elin noticed that the Three Companions possessed a quality of stillness. She describes it as 'letting things emerge and not trying to influence too much; an inviting'. I think this is a beautiful connection. Lottie felt, 'Those three combined would paint a picture of somebody who you can look up to. They're inspirational. You can ask them for advice.' This explanation has a mentoring quality to it, while Milly felt that we can get by without being wise ourselves because we can draw on the wisdom of others. I think this is partly true; we can do that in the short term, but this does not allow us to achieve our full potential.

In that respect, Phyllis captured the reason why I set up the CCW Community in March 2020:

COVID is a perfect example of how you can put these three into practice. You need to have compassion for other people, you simply can't be so self-absorbed and think that you're the only one who is undergoing all the things that you're going through. If you can begin to see how other people are facing similar – maybe even worse – issues, that may give you the courage to do certain things outside yourself. I think that together how courage and compassion impact the decisions you make, and the outcomes that might result from those decisions, will ultimately result in wisdom. If you can open yourself up to the lessons that are coming, these three work well together, to make you a fuller person and give you the things that you need.

In Part Two: Displaying Courage, Compassion and Wisdom, we can read about the situations in which individuals did and did not employ the Three Companions and see how we relate to these. Before we do that, I would like to share with you a visual representation of how I see the Three Companions working together.

Finding an ideal
way of being

I see the Three Companions as virtues that are additive to and reinforcing of each other. The metaphor that depicts this is a triple-stranded helix. I did some research on the topic 'triple helix' and discovered a couple of examples that I would like to share with you:

- In nature, this form can be found in collagen (a protein in our bodies). I am no biologist but understand that the triple helical structure provides strength and stability to collagen fibres.
- The Triple Helix Model of Innovation describes the relationships between academia, governments and industry to promote economic and social development.[9] I spoke with Professor Loet Leydesdorff, one of the creators of the model, to get a better understanding of it. He told me that the purpose of the relationship between any three variables is synergy.

I hold that the aspects of strength, stability and synergy can be applied to the Three Companions.

Like the Model of Innovation, each virtue can have a linear relationship with another: courage–wisdom, courage–compassion, compassion–wisdom. Courage enables us to stand alone and share our truth. Wisdom ameliorates bravery so we are not rash in our courage.

As we discovered earlier, courage enables us to witness and be alongside another's pain. And compassion can give us the courage to fight against injustices. Wisdom allows us to find the right way to express our compassion while being with others in their suffering increases our wisdom. However, the Three Companions together create synergy. The roles, that these three play, change through their interactions over time. They continually evolve the way that we engage with our world, leading to positive change.

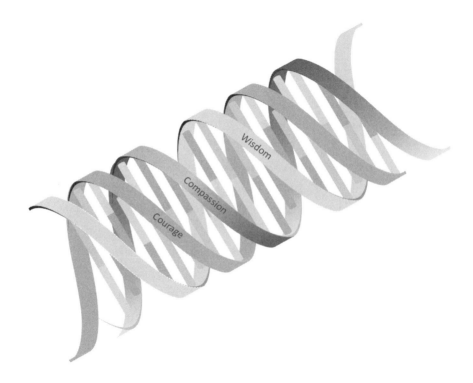

This framework is flexible enough to allow each of us to develop a way of expressing and combining each quality that is uniquely ours. I think that the most powerful approach is in some form of learning community in which you can share your ideas and experiences, hear from others and experiment with new behaviours. Reflective practice is an important element here.

The stories that follow in Part Two are designed to help us to reflect on our own circumstances, how we typically respond to situations and what we might do differently based on what we take from them. In Part Three, I go into more depth about the practices that enhance our ability to employ the Three Companions more freely.

2

DISPLAYING COURAGE, COMPASSION AND WISDOM

The Three Companions show up in a range of scenarios in our personal and work lives. In fact, there are countless opportunities every day to use them in our relationships with ourselves and others, whether it is to counteract our inner critic and show ourselves compassion, or to interact with others in a way that leads to the best possible outcome over time.

During my interviews, one of my observations was that many people struggled to find stories depicting all three qualities. I encouraged my interviewees to start with the Companion that resonated the most with them. Often, we then discovered the presence of all three of the Companions in those situations that they described as using one or two of them. So, during the interviews, we evolved our understanding of how the Three Companions might act in concert, and my participants learnt how courage, compassion and wisdom were already manifest in themselves. It seems that we are unused to reflecting on how these virtues show up in us.

As you read the stories that follow, I invite you to consider which Companions you can detect or would probe for if you were the interviewer. You may choose to read through the scenarios in order or jump to the one that speaks to you and/or resonates with your circumstances. The categories are:

- educating and developing yourself
- replenishing yourself
- coping with illness
- the final moments of someone's life
- parenting
- handling strains in relationships
- helping others
- protecting and defending others
- dealing with crises
- resolving dilemmas with integrity and ethics
- challenging power
- leading people through change.

I encourage you to immerse yourself in these stories, notice how you feel and why. Take this opportunity to imagine, or remember, yourself in similar circumstances. What would you choose to do now you've learnt about the Three Companions?

Educating and developing yourself

It can take a lot of courage, compassion and wisdom to develop ourselves. I know from my own experiences that I undergo a lot of growth when I uncover things about myself that were not in my consciousness before – particularly those negative traits or emotions that I experience and then examine what they mean.

I have, for example, long held the belief that it is not good to express my anger by losing control and shouting at people. I have prided myself on being able to reflect on what I want to say and respond calmly. What I did not realise was that at times my response was to go into a cold rage in which I would not express my feelings, but they would eat away at me. I would ruminate for hours about the situation and argue with myself that I should let it go and be understanding of the other person. I have been disappointed with myself that my good intentions of not expressing my anger or impatience with a situation have not led to my displaying courage, compassion and wisdom. Instead, my anger has leaked out in my nonverbal communication and, worse still, in passive-aggressive behaviour. Confronting this and learning more about myself takes courage and self-compassion and increases my wisdom.

Here are some stories from individuals who showed elements of the Three Companions through either gaining an education or developing themselves in some way. One that particularly struck me was an experience of Grace, who introduced me to the unfamiliar world of growing up in Africa:

I define it as courage now, but it didn't feel like that then; it was a decision I needed to make. My parents separated when I was too young to know. I stayed with my mum until I was primary school age. At this point, my mum had had four kids. I'd been going to school and doing well. So, the teacher said to her that the only way I could get good primary leaving exam scores was if I went to boarding school. My mum couldn't afford it. My father had a bit of money so she sent me to my father to say, 'Could he pay for my school fees?' I think, as adults, they hadn't agreed, so they had their issues. My dad says, 'I can't talk about that', and sends me back.

To walk from my mum's to my dad's was maybe 30 minutes. That for an African is OK. We lived in the same vicinity. So, he sends me off with a few words, she sends me back with a few words. And I go back the third time to my dad's, and he says, 'I will not pay for a child who lives in another man's house.'

My mum was living by herself with my siblings. My father translates that as she has a relationship. Anyway, it's: 'I'm not contributing to somebody else. If they are my kids, they need to be with me.' And my mother was saying, 'I'm not giving my children to another woman. I can raise my children.' So, I went from my dad; I knew what my mother would say, I went halfway between them and stood in a corner. I was about probably eight or nine. I stood and hid in a corner somewhere where nobody would see me. I knew if somebody saw me, they would tell my mum, 'Oh, we saw your daughter', or my dad, 'We saw your daughter just standing', or they would walk with me because, in an African place, everybody's your keeper.

So, I stood there and counted in my head what I think would be the right time to have gone to my dad, had a conversation, and then gone back. I went back to my mum and said to her, 'Listen, I'm going to pack up my things. I'm going to go and stay with my dad. That's what I prefer to do.'

My father had a TV, and he was the only one that had a TV at that point. He had a house that had two rooms and a tiny store. He was considered rich, and he had a telly within this slum. My mum lived in one room with about ten people. So, she's thinking, 'This nine-year-old has decided that she wants to go to a place where they are rich and have a TV.'

Very far from my thoughts. I'm thinking, 'I need an education. The only way I'm going to get an education is if my father pays for me. The only way he pays for me is if I live with him, and my mother will not agree to this. So, I'm going to choose and throw myself on the ground.' I said to her, 'Listen, I'm going to go', and she's like, 'You've chosen your father because he's got lots of money.' I said, 'No, but I'll go and stay with him for a bit.' Then I packed up. I went and stayed with my father. He started to pay my fees. My decision was, 'I need school fees; I can't be dealing with these two people going back and forth.'

We can see the courage, compassion, and wisdom that it took for Grace to make the decision to go and live with her father. The magnitude of this becomes evident as she continues her story:

It was hard being a stepchild; there's always this stepchild–stepmother relationship: impossible. My stepmother did all sorts. You come to their house to become their maid and that's what it is. Even at a young age, I quickly worked out that I needed to survive. There's no other way. What are you going to do about it? I would wake up in the morning before everybody. I wasn't the oldest, she had two kids older than me, but they would still be sleeping. I would wake up and do all the chores. I knew to be on good behaviour so that I could survive. And that was it. And she did all sorts of things. So, it wasn't a good place to be. But I needed school fees and that was it. Do the chores. Get your school fees.

Grace's experience in growing up was so different to mine. I thought her story epitomised the Three Companions, yet she felt that it was nothing special. That was just how they had to live.

Another glimpse into a different world came from Gloria, who grew up in a large family in the Caribbean and was sent away to boarding school:

I had my first introduction to courage when my mother decided that she wanted me to be a lady, and she sent me to a school 40 miles away. I think she had a premonition that she was going to die. She put me with a regular 'blue stocking', who was very strict. I was very unhappy, but I had to keep courage because I felt that that's what my mother wanted. I didn't want to let her down.

One of the things about school was that we didn't get a lot to eat. When I came home for school holidays, on Sunday mornings, there was usually a big spread for breakfast of about a dozen things on the table! I'd be eating and she'd be putting her hand on her chest, 'Oh, my poor child has been starving.' I was pleased to hear that, and I would eat more! But she still sent me back until three months before she died. However, she didn't send me there for the last Christmas term before she died in March 1948. I was not yet 12 years old and spent the last three months of my mother's life going to the local school. That was my first experience of courage!

In this snippet we do not glimpse compassion and wisdom; however, I suspect that aspects of all Three Companions were being used.

In this next story, Lida moved from the Czech Republic to the UK to get her education. This required her to show enormous courage, compassion and wisdom:

Courage would go all the way back to when I came to the UK. I originally came for three months to improve my English. I wanted to be an English and literature teacher. I really wanted to do that. I'm from a tiny village where nobody ever left, and everybody still lives with their parents. It's a nice, close community. But I always wanted to travel. I always wanted to do something a little different, and I enjoyed languages.

One of my teachers kept encouraging us. He used to say, 'If you're studying a language, go and practise it. Sitting at home, reading books in that language is not going to make you talk.' He always told us, 'Just go and talk. Don't worry about making mistakes. Don't worry about people laughing at you. Because those who laugh at you, you don't want to be talking to those people anyway. And those who understand how hard it is to learn another language, they will help you. These are the people you surround yourself with.'

I knew I was making mistakes when I was speaking English, but I thought, 'I'm only going to get better if I continue trying.'

When I was about to leave the UK, I realised that I could do my degree there. For me, that was courageous simply because I promised my mum I was definitely coming back home. In the Czech Republic, it's not common for kids to move away for uni or anything. So, by turning around to my mum and saying, 'You know I said I was going for three months? I am now going to stay on and do my degree'. And then putting myself through uni and working full time, not relying on anybody, I thought I was being fairly courageous. I know it's a common thing you hear, but I come from an environment where this is not very common. I still see it as one of my biggest achievements. I always knew that the Czech Republic is slightly behind because we were behind the Iron Curtain until '89. So, we didn't have many influences from the outside. I only knew this the first time I was able to travel out with my dad. We were only allowed to travel together; the rest of the family couldn't come. So, we had massive restrictions. Even when the political situation changed, we were still catching up.

So, I was one of the first people who left and made something out of it. I'm hoping that's going to inspire others. I've got two little cousins who just turned ten. I hope that they are not going to see it as courageous; they will see it as normal.

I believe that it took a lot of courage for Lida to move from the sheltered life in her village in the Czech Republic to bustling, and often unfriendly, London. I see elements of wisdom in that she understood the benefits of gaining an education in the UK compared to the less worldly view she would have gained if she had returned home to study. Lida wanted to be a role model, which is so important in helping other people to see what's possible.

We can identify that Lida acted with courage and wisdom in her decision to stay in the UK. Compassion made its appearance in how she maintained contact with her mother with frequent messages and phone calls, and trips home every six months. A poignant moment in her story was that her mother became very ill while she was home for a visit. This was the last semester of her degree. Lida was all set to move back home to be with her mother when her father challenged her thinking:

My dad looked at me and said, 'So, three years of studying exams, late nights, working around your uni hours, and you're gonna give it all up in the last semester.'

And I was looking at him: 'Well, Mum is ill, and she needs me here.'

And he goes, 'Yeah, but she also has got me. She's got your brother. You will be coming home. It would be really stupid to throw away three years of hard work, knowing how much you've put into it.' That was nice, my dad having my back like that. Even though I know my mum probably gave him a proper talking to, she wouldn't want me to return for the wrong reasons either.

This illustrates one of the domains that helps us to use the Three Companions: a support network can help us to figure out what we are going to do when we are facing difficult situations. In this case, it was a direct challenge. At other times, it can be enough to have a listening, non-judgemental ear. We will need distinctive kinds of support at different times. Knowing what support we need, and who can provide it, is one factor that allows us to be more intentional in using the Three Companions.

Anna showed enormous courage in moving countries to pursue further study at the height of her professional career:

I think sometimes it's good to stretch yourself and not just be in a comfort zone and do nothing. I wanted to do this new area of psychology when nobody knew anything about it. I knew in my heart – you can call it God, or you can call it wisdom, you can call it anything – but I knew in my heart I needed to do that. I had quit my job and had no savings. I had a little girl. And I had to go all the way to America, which was a place that I'd never been. I was an introvert and would never go anywhere by myself, especially to new places where I didn't know anybody.

Even attending the class was challenging. This was an Ivy League school. Not only was everyone taller than me, whiter than me, somehow, when you come from a developing country, there's a distance between them and you. I felt it so much because in my class there were best-selling authors, heirs of luminaries, and even a transplant surgeon. They were all kinds of everything. And who was I? This little person from an Asian country, just an HR consultant who wanted to learn. Also, these people had come from Stanford, Yale, Harvard – and I came from where? An Australian university. I came from such a different world. And I was thrown in at the deep end.

On the first day we had to introduce ourselves. We did it in pairs. When the professor asked, 'Who has heard an interesting story?', the person I was talking to put up her hand. And she said, 'I was talking to Anna. She's from Asia, and she's never been to America. This is her first trip out here. I think she's so brave to come all this distance and live here by herself.' And so, I had to get up and address the very class that I was so afraid of.

Anna's back story is fascinating. As a teenager, she had wanted to become a church pastor but coming from a non-religious family, that was not an option. Anna's pastor gave her this advice: 'You have brains. Here in Church, we have many people. Go use your brain out there in the world. The world shall be your ministry.' That has stuck with her all her life. Anna then decided to become a psychologist to make people's lives better, but that too was discouraged by her father. It was many years before she could study psychology as an undergraduate and continue with her Masters at the American university. Anna's wisdom was knowing that this was the right thing for her to do and would be successful. Her family, particularly her then 8-year-old daughter, showed her compassion by giving her their blessings.

Maja also moved countries to further her career:

Aged 15, I came on holiday [to England] with my mother and auditioned at drama schools. I was accepted and told my mother that I wanted to stay. So, my mother went home to Canada, alone. This was in July 1975; I turned 16 in September. I wanted so much to be an actor over here. In the early days I felt very alone and had some problems with accommodation. Looking back, it was incredibly tough. Then I moved into a bedsit in Chiswick and stayed there for five years, which gave me some stability. I had a passion for the profession. I was a child actor; my parents were in the business. It's in my blood. I wanted to be in this amazing country with all its theatres. It was passion that enabled me to do this. I could have gone home at any time.

I suspect there was some wisdom in knowing that staying in the UK would give her lots of opportunities to grow as an actor.

Another example about moving countries for professional development is from Eleni:

> I always think of this when I'm thinking good things about myself. I was really courageous. When I was about 42 or 43, my work as an actor had dried up after a really successful period. I had gone for about two years, and I wasn't getting any work, or dribs and drabs. So, I retrained as a teacher and went to live in Italy. I basically went with 200 euros and a suitcase. I did have a place to live because the school provided that. I learnt the language. I learnt about the culture. I outgrew the schools that I was working in and the little towns I lived in. I moved to bigger and bigger towns, then into a small city and then set up my own business. When that didn't serve me anymore, I came back to the UK and picked up my acting career again. I'm quite proud of myself for that. I think that was brave.

Eleni showed great strength in taking this action. Eleni reflected that at the time she was feeling bitter and twisted, and jealous of more successful actors. Eleni felt this was a position of weakness. So going to Italy was an act of resistance and defiance. Her wisdom now tells her that if she could have relaxed, she would have been able to get what she wanted in London. Yet it is difficult to know what would have happened. Eleni is a different person now. I suspect that she could not have seen her situation in any other way then.

I infer from Eleni's story that there was wisdom in knowing that she needed an alternative means of generating income. There was an element of self-compassion in noticing how she was feeling; she was aware of negative emotions: 'I think I was aware of it at the time even though I was inside of it.'

Growth often comes when we intentionally take courageous action to face up to who we are, what has led us to this point in our life journey, and what else we need to do. The next two stories are about decisions that people took to allow themselves to continue a journey of self-discovery and being themselves.

The first is from Hugo. He had experienced significant trauma in his early life. He chose to become a monk partly so as not to pass on the results of his trauma to potential children. Having started on his path of emotional healing, decades later Hugo wanted to speed up this process and so chose to leave his life as a monk:

Choosing to leave my monkship was a courageous act. I always had a desire to be free of the burdens and shackles of the discipline, but part of me remained strongly dedicated. Therefore, I meant to see it through as a lifelong commitment.

As my self-awareness grew over the years, I reached the point of deciding to undergo psychotherapy. Through this I became more aware of the early-life trauma I had experienced in my household. I came to realise that part of my decision to become a monk had been to avoid intimacy, which gave me an easy track to avoid the difficulties and challenges of intimate relationships. I had always operated in a role. Informal, unstructured conversation had always been very difficult for me and made me feel very nervous. While growing up, the world had often seemed fretful and fearful for me.

As I became aware of my trauma, I could understand it from a different perspective and see that there was real scope for healing and recovery. I assessed that the biggest deficit hampering me was a lack of belief in myself and my worthiness as a human being. In my infancy, my mum became ill and went to the hospital. While she was away, relatives came over to care for me and my siblings. This occurred in the fifties when there was a common and horrible practice to let babies cry to teach them not to do so. Somewhere in my cells, I have a lingering sense of having been left alone for a long time. I cried in desperation and was calling out, crying out, for somebody, for 'them', for anyone, to come and be with me. But nobody came. I cried more and more, louder and louder, with more and more desperation. And then something inside me broke. I realised that: 'They are not coming because I'm not good enough. I'm wrong. Something about me is "made wrong".' And that has been a lifelong, deeply embedded belief.

When I reflect on my early experiences, I believe that even after my mum came back, I couldn't open up to trust others. Having been abandoned was too obliteratingly painful. I think that is what caused me to have difficulty in relationships. My parents' marriage broke up when I was still a toddler. So, I had a disbelief in my ability to forge a good relationship and carry on with it. It might break up like my parents had. And maybe I would have children that would undergo the same shock and trauma as I had undergone. I didn't want to do that.

So, in my late teens when I came across some spiritual teachings which I liked and the scope to be a monk, it felt like something beautiful to step into. I spent several deeply meaningful decades as a monk. Fast-forward to the years of my therapy, I reasoned that if I stayed as a monk, it would probably take me the rest of my life to work through my early-life trauma. If I left, however, I assessed I could likely do it in a lot less time. So I chose to leave.

It was a courageous and compassionate move based on the wisdom that he had at that time. He has since learnt more about trauma and had cutting-edge treatment that he now believes he could have had without leaving that spiritual community. That said, this wisdom enabled him to form the most intimate of relationships; he got married seven years after leaving his monkship.

The second story was told to me by Javier, who had hidden his homosexuality until he was 21. The story begins with his fear of how others might react to him:

God, the biggest one [example of not displaying the Three Companions] would be not coming out until I was bloody 21. That's the one that will never leave me. That's the one tinged in the most guilt. I was just wishing it would go away. I was thinking it wasn't permanent, possible, or realistic; not seeing anyone who looked like me who was openly gay. I think I was worrying what other people would think; that was probably the main thing.

Then Javier stepped into his fear and showed great courage, compassion and wisdom in disclosing to his dying mother that he was gay:

I think I only came out because when Mum's cancer came back in the summer before she passed away, I thought, 'I can't not be open about this while someone who means so much to me is still here, doesn't know what I've been going through and may not have much more time.' I thought, 'I have to do, with what I have left timewise, what I need.' And that involved being myself. I don't even like the terminology 'coming out', because I think: 'Why don't straight people have to come out? Why is it only gay people who have to state their sexual preference?' That was a real turning point. The decision was taken out of my hands, really. I felt I could not, not make that decision. That's what I meant by the decision was taken out of my hands. It was the only thing I could do.

When I asked, 'So, what were you worried about or scared about?' Javier replied:

Not fitting in, not being accepted, not accepting myself. Thinking, 'If I'm having such a big deal with this, how are other people in my life gonna manage this?' And, quite frankly, a lot of negative messaging about the life I could have led, the life of gay black people. Direct phrases from people in my life who'd suggested that it wouldn't be me. They were not saying, 'You can't be gay because we think you're not gay', because, apparently, no one knew for some reason. I don't know how no one knew. I don't know how no one saw someone so anxious and so unhappy. I just felt like I was reeking of discomfort in myself, and I don't know how I managed to not let that come across. I think the other reason why that didn't come out sooner was a profound belief that I couldn't be happy while being that openly gay.

Javier's first experience of disclosing that he was gay did not go well. Therefore, it is unsurprising that he chose to bury it for a few more years. It also highlights how courageous Javier was when he did eventually tell his mother:

Who did I come out to first? I came out to a few people while I was at university with terrible – well, not terrible – consequences, but just shock and 'That can't be true!' And I thought, 'Oh, shit! OK, well, better not try that again.' So, I buried it for a few more years. Then I eventually told a teacher who has now become a close friend.

Javier shows profound wisdom and compassion in his telling of his mother's reaction to his news:

It's really difficult. I want to be truthful and honest about it. It wasn't negative, but the first reaction was, 'Well, are you sure? I had no idea.' I caught her off-guard, apparently. And eventually the: 'I love you. It doesn't matter to me.' You almost want someone to know what you're talking about first because their split-second reaction is not necessarily going to be what they would have wanted that interaction to be like. I'm sure if Mum could have rewritten that whole story, it would have involved her reacting in the way that she did three, four minutes after I told her.

On the whole, it was a good reaction. She was also really supportive. To be honest, she was too unwell at that point to be what I needed for those last few months, but at least I did get to tell her. So yeah, it was courage. That probably will be the defining moment of courage.

Replenishing yourself

The stories featured in this chapter are about individuals who experienced distressing and/or demanding times and who had to find their way through them – hence the need to replenish themselves. I think it is so important to replenish so that we can be present with ourselves and others in times of need. If we don't, we run the risk of sacrificing ourselves and feeling depleted or worse. Sometimes, we just need a few moments for ourselves and that is enough for us to recharge our batteries. At other times, we want the help of people who understand us and can be there for us. Only we can know what is right for us.

I personally replenish myself through expression and conversation. I have been through a gruelling time over the last few years. My husband died in February 2020 and a few weeks later we went into lockdown due to COVID-19. The last two years of his life were particularly difficult because he abused alcohol to cope with a lot of unhappiness in his life. This affected his mood and behaviour, and I suffered too as a result. I turned to close family and friends for support. A few lived through my distress with me, and others have empathised with me since his death. And I have sought therapy to make sense of my experience. All these connections have greatly helped me to retain equanimity, name my feelings and alleviate my pain.

Another story that illustrates the importance of self-care through replenishing ourselves was told to me by Elin, who had discovered her husband was having an affair. He had had at least three affairs over 25 years of marriage; this latest one had lasted for more than five years. After various attempts to save their marriage failed, they became legally separated. Elin described to me how she was able to show him compassion:

My example of compassion comes from my personal life. It evolved and emerged during and after the break-up of my marriage. I find that I have been able to be generous in spirit towards my ex-husband.

I made a promise to myself that I would try and get through this with grace. I think I failed at that. My attempt to get through it with grace was about my own self-preservation. But I think in failing at grace, compassion towards myself and my ex-husband turned up.

I wanted to rise above it and be compassionate and wise and all that, and I couldn't. I was too hurt. By hurt I don't just mean I felt hurt. I did feel tremendously hurt but, also, I was angry, sad. I felt vindictive and a mixture of highly energised, mostly very unpleasant impulses, emotions and thoughts.

I couldn't hold on to the grace and not succumb to all those impulses, thoughts and emotions. In grace there is also a strength to not succumb, so that I wouldn't be emotionally destroyed. What I found was that I had to accept all that about myself, and then I was a lot kinder to myself, which I guess would be self-compassion. Once I found that, it was really easy to extend it. It was just normal, natural, and much easier than trying to fend off all these impulses and emotions. I think I'd misunderstood grace, but I do remember working really hard on it.

When I asked, 'What enabled you to express yourself as you are and start to be kind to yourself?' Elin replied:

A couple of things. I had some individual counselling. I kept confessing to my counsellor all these things I was thinking and wanting to do, and ways I was behaving. And she kept saying, 'That's normal. That's normal. That's normal. In these circumstances, that's normal.' It was a bit of a worn-out record, 'this is normal'.

She didn't ever say, 'You have to start thinking about this in a different way.' But I did start thinking about it differently. Because I would feel a feeling arising and I would think, 'Oh, well, she said, "That's normal."' And when I think about my own experience, working with people in distress, of course that's normal. Why wouldn't I apply that to myself? Then I got quite quickly to a point where I could feel the feeling coming or see the thought heating, or whatever it was, and I would think, 'Oh, yeah, that's just that. That's just that I want to murder her. If I was doing it in my fantasy life, this is exactly how I would do it. And this is how it would play out. That's just that.' And not waste a whole lot of energy on trying to not think it or feel guilty about it.

Also, I started to write a novel about it, which meant that I was bathing in it. I was inserting myself into the fantasy. The novel opens with the beginning of my first interview by a forensic psychiatrist in the old psychiatric hospital where I used to work. There's this elaborate series of murders that I've done.'

The key to Elin being able to show compassion was having her experience normalised. She learnt to recognise and acknowledge her feelings without over-identifying with them or suppressing them, which is an element of self-compassion. We also talked about the importance of establishing personal boundaries. She explained:

It's interesting, knowing the boundary thing. Until I had got to a point of self-compassion, I don't think the boundary thing was very clear to me at all. Then it was much easier to do, to have a boundary. When there were tricky interactions with my ex-husband, I could actually say to myself, 'Oh, that's him. That's not me.' Or, 'This is the me that I'm going to bring into this interaction.' A lot of other stuff fell away. It was much easier. And it's been easier ever since. That's interesting. I don't think he's got that for himself, which is quite sad. Not that we have these conversations, but I can tell. Whereas our children say to me that in some ways, I seem quite different now.

Lily experienced rage when she found out that her husband was having an emotional affair at the time that she was recovering from her breast cancer (see page 68). Like Elin, she had fantasies where she was violent to this other woman:

I had an emotional affair with this person. A year or so later, my husband also had an emotional affair. There was nothing physical going on. I guess these people came into our lives and were offering us a connection. But initially, I felt so much anger towards this lady who had come into my husband's life.

I was so incredibly angry, I didn't even recognise myself. I thought, 'What she's done is unforgivable. She's preyed on this weak situation; I've got no boobs, no hair.' I thought it was the lowest of low behaviour from this lady. As time's gone on, I slowly recognised that we were probably the same. We were probably behaving in the same way because we thought we needed attention. I identified a lot of the behaviour in myself. So, I think I was angrier at myself because I thought, 'Well, she's such a terrible person. That makes me a terrible person.'

My counsellor said, 'We can only do the best we can with the resources we have at the time.' Now, if I'm feeling like I'm feeling unloved, I'm honest about it with my husband and I talk about it because that's a better way to deal with those feelings.

Lily learnt to use her Three Companions to express her emotions and her needs, rather than look for solace outside her marriage. She told me that her husband's affair was the start of redressing the balance in their relationship. Lily was reminded that they are both fallible human beings, rather than she being the one who was flawed and incompetent. When I asked her about her anger, she said:

It's anger like I've never known. Lots of shouting. Lots of talking to myself. I would drive past where she worked. For me, it was very visionary. I had visions of wanting to hurt her. Going to her place of work and grabbing her by the hair and slamming her head into a desk. Driving past her place of work and calling her all manner of names out loud.

I asked her, 'I'm wondering what was behind the anger?'
Lily replied:

I was still very much in the early stages of recovery and dealing with all the trauma of breast cancer. But I think it stems from fear. The fear that our family wasn't working out and it was just all such a big mess.

Lily's story supports the view of Elin's counsellor that these fantasies and feelings are normal.

Peter felt that he and his wife had grown apart and he showed himself enough self-compassion to say, 'This is not what I want.' At the same time, he questioned whether he could have shown more compassion towards his wife, who was deeply hurt:

For me it was, I don't want to have a relationship with a woman whom I love very much and want to do everything with, but like brother and sister, where you have lost interest in each other's activities. For example, there were no sports anymore that we did together. That's just one example. I

think in a relationship, you need to have a few things where you say, 'Wow, that's nice. We would like to do that together.'

I asked him, 'What do you think would have happened if you had stayed in that brother–sister type of relationship?'
He said:

I think we would have had many good and bad conversations. Maybe some parts would have improved. But there was also a great difference between us in how we looked at sex. There was no moving towards me. And it was not the situation that I wanted to do it twice a day or seven times a week. But there was difference between us. If you want to improve a situation it needs to come from both sides.

Of course, it was compassion for myself. I feel pain. I want to get rid of it. So, I need to be compassionate towards myself. The wisdom was there and, on the other hand, I could also say there was no wisdom because: *Why haven't you tried more? Why haven't you tried years before to start a conversation? Haven't you noticed that we were diverging rather than converging?* And compassion – there should have been more compassion towards my wife.

I think I didn't have the courage to start the difficult conversation with my wife when I realised we were growing apart. Instead of that, I started a relationship. During that affair I didn't have the courage to tell my wife about it. When everything came out, I had the courage to start [counselling] sessions together with my wife to find out whether we could continue our relationship. And, if not, then we would learn a lot about ourselves and our relationship. After counselling I realised there was no future for our marriage, so I decided to divorce. I think courage, self-compassion and wisdom came together with that decision.

Another example of turning to a professional for support was shared by Faith, who wanted to support her daughter who was facing trial for drug dealing. Faith was getting advice from a lot of people that went against her gut instincts. She was unsure about trusting her intuition, so she sought out various support groups until she found a counsellor who was experienced in helping people with drug-related problems. She told me:

The general advice you hear in those situations is to let them go. Let them sort out what it is. Don't accept that behaviour in the house. They have to sink or swim, sort themselves out. I wasn't in for that. Instead, I contacted lots of help groups and finally got to him [the counsellor].

Even though I didn't learn anything new, he helped me put words on the situation: 'No, you can't throw someone out of the house. It's not good to do that.' Every time that there was disagreement between my husband and myself, we would go back to the man. My husband would say, 'I think we should throw her out. It's the only way.' And he would say, 'I don't think so. Where would she go? What would she do?' I used that man – so that I could get the right wording, the patience and take the fear out of it all – to follow my own advice.

I took a chance going there, and he said, 'No, you can't do that, wherever would they go? They'd just get worse. You wouldn't know what situations they'd get into then.' That was one fear; it would be much worse for her. Then, there was the fear of what would happen in the court cases, but you just had to take courage in both your hands and just keep going. I used a higher power trust at that point as well. And it did work out to keep going. I got the courage to keep going by trusting.

Maeve suffered from a period of deep depression and turned to a counsellor for support. She found the courage to deal with everything and keep going through the help of that counsellor:

> This time last year, I had very bad depression. Through counselling, various things that happened in my life and various friends, I found this courage. I'm turning my life around. I'm moving to a different area. I've got some new friends. A lot of things have changed. If I looked at myself this time last year, there is no way I could have done that. I think that takes courage and belief in yourself.

She and her counsellor spent a lot of time talking about compassion. Through their interactions she discovered that she was very compassionate towards others but very hard on herself. She was always comparing herself unfavourably to others. The counselling enabled her to show self-compassion and feel happier in herself.

To be able to demonstrate courage, compassion and wisdom requires energy and this may deplete our reserves. It is important that we take care of ourselves by taking time to replenish them. Idris illustrates this beautifully:

> For me, it's very simple things, actually. It's exercise. I know I have to physically keep my energy up and going. The other thing that really helps – so in my last two careers, I've had lots of travel; airports and airplanes are good places to re-energise. You have to resist the temptation to work all the time. Instead, I have to say, 'You know what, I'm just gonna listen to some Miles Davis', or 'I'm going to take this hour to snooze', or 'I'm just going to read an interesting book. I'm gonna turn off my mind and not feel guilty about it.' Because it's easy to start feeling guilty that you're being selfish in some ways. But I know that I need that in order to be there for other people.

Asking for help is a sign of strength, although many of us see this as an indication of weakness. Recognising that we cannot solve our problems alone and showing our vulnerability to others takes courage, (self-)compassion and wisdom. Leya reflected on how she bore the responsibility for taking care of her parents and sister. She felt resentful that this burden had rested solely on her shoulders. Leya realised that she had contributed to this situation by not asking her siblings for help. She used that insight to ask her children to share the responsibility, with her, for taking care of their own brother since he too needed help:

My sister died a couple weeks ago. Over the last 12 years, I have had the financial responsibility to make sure there was enough money to take care of her, pay her bills and everything else. It was a significant responsibility and got more so as she became more and more dysfunctional. I had been taking care of my parents, and then my sister, for a total of 30 years.

When my sister died, it gave me an opportunity for reflection because this was clearly an end to an era. I had spent many years being very frustrated with my siblings. They had allowed me to be the responsible one and they'd never stepped up. I even had one sister who had written to me when my mother died and said, 'We really appreciate all you did for Mum and Dad for the last 20 years. We could have done more; we just didn't want to.' Which I thought was a terrible thing to say. How could you say that? 'We could have but we didn't.' But in thinking about it, I learnt a lesson: 'Wait a minute, I went through 30 years of being frustrated that they weren't helping, but did I ever ask? Did I ever raise the boundary and say, "Hey, guys, there are eight of us here, not just one? We are collectively responsible for Mum and Dad. We are collectively responsible for this sister who can't take care of herself. This is not about me; this is about us. What are we doing about it?"' I never asked. I assumed that I needed to do it.

I have a son who's chronically ill, who I've been taking care of for the last few years and paying his bills. I called my children for a family council. They're all adults. I said, 'Guys, this is a collective responsibility. The truth is, I need your help. I'm getting older. You can't drive him to his appointments or help when he's in the emergency room or whatever. And you can't help him emotionally, other than to call him and talk to him, because you're not here. I have to do all of that myself. I need your help with the things you can help with. We need to figure out what they are. We need to schedule them. We need to make it work.' It was so freeing because I didn't say, 'You're horrible people.' I practised self-compassion: 'I will not allow you to abdicate the responsibility the way my siblings did. We're going to work this out together.' They were a lot more willing to help and a lot better at what they came up with than I had expected.

So often, we make assumptions about what the outcome will be. So we don't exercise the courage to try a different approach. We've already written in our mind what the answer is going to be from those people. We don't give them the opportunity to also practise courage, wisdom and compassion. I believe people are better than we think they are. Given the opportunity to exercise courage, compassion and wisdom, they will – particularly if we can set an example and help them understand what's needed.

I think Leya's last statement is so true. How often do we pre-empt the reactions and responses of others? Or decide that they have enough on their plate, and we don't want to burden them with our troubles? We return to the practices of highly resilient people. One of these is generosity, i.e., helping others increases our resilience.[10] By requesting help, we are giving others a gift.

Coping with illness

No matter how much we embrace life in its fullness, it is often scary to face sickness of any kind. I think that dealing with illness is a time when we need the Three Companions. I imagine that we all know of individuals who have suffered from a dramatic change in their life circumstances. Sometimes, they have recovered fully from this, and in other cases, sadly they have not. We cannot guarantee that we will always be able to live the life we want and do the things that we enjoy. Illness covers all aspects of health – physical, psychological, emotional, spiritual, social. I remember how I used the Three Companions when facing the possibility of cancer...

I am fortunate that I have enjoyed good health in all respects for most of my life. So when something feels wrong, it is worrying. I tend to leave it for some time before I consult a general practitioner to see if it disappears. When I had ovarian cysts, it took courage to face the possibility that they were malignant and all that would entail. I was kind to myself and to my husband, who was annoyed with himself for dismissing my concerns. The wisdom lay in trusting the expert and knowing that I would face the news at each stage. It was also about not worrying my mother and children unnecessarily but sharing the news with them when I knew the full diagnosis.

Amongst my interviewees, there were many stories about coping with illness – either their own or of those closest to them. For the most part, the stories were about displaying courage, compassion and wisdom in these difficult circumstances. Phyllis, for example, talked at length about coping with her breast cancer. She did not want this experience to define her and realised that in the past she might have minimised or suppressed what she went through. She was surprised at how much she needed to share this story in its entirety, telling me:

In 2018, I was diagnosed with breast cancer, stage two, and I had to undergo various treatments. I had a lumpectomy, radiation, and chemo. That was a period where I felt courage, compassion and wisdom were coming to bear. Courage was something I had to display because I am essentially a private person. I wanted to go through my experience privately, but chemo didn't allow for that. I grappled with that for a while. When I shaved my head, the question was 'Do I buy a wig?', which I wore once or twice, but it didn't feel authentic. Then I tried the scarf; that was itchy and uncomfortable. I felt that the best way forward for me was to be bald. I wasn't prepared to deal with all the questions and stares. So, it took me a while to figure out what I was going to do. I thought, 'I'm going to face scrutiny, but this is what it is. How can I simultaneously take the attention away from me and yet make something good out of this situation?'

I researched some charities and then selected Cancer Research Malaysia. I approached them about my situation and told them that I would like to raise funds for them. I launched an Indiegogo campaign and put this together while undergoing treatment. Once I had done this, I felt more positive about my situation and able to make good use of the attention that would come my way. When I launched the campaign, I announced it on social media. I opened up, told my story and asked people to support me by donating to a good cause. All the funds raised went straight to that research foundation. I raised just under 2,000 US dollars, which I felt was a good result. My chemo took approximately six months, and I wanted a finite timeframe to do this. At the end of six months, the campaign ended, and I gave all the money to the foundation.

When I shared my story, I saw compassion over and over. The CEO of the foundation said, 'We need more people like you to come forward and share your story. Many people are in denial when they face situations like this. They don't want to deal with it. They don't get tested. By the time they finally act, it's too late.'

So I recorded a short video at home. I wanted it to be as authentic as possible. Many friends, colleagues and connections, near and far, wished me well. The support kept flooding in. I was frankly amazed at the outpouring. The support helped me through such a dark period. What I took away from that situation is that sometimes you have to put yourself out there – and you have to trust. I did that, and friends and family were around to provide support.

I was invited to speak at a big conference locally and this coincided with the end of my six cycles. Typically, you feel completely drained and lifeless for the first week post-chemo. So, I was hesitant about accepting that invitation. Yet I also saw it as a good opportunity to take my message out in a bigger way. The conference organiser was apprised of my situation and was thankfully understanding. He said, 'Just go with how you feel. If at that time you feel that you really can't make it, then I will understand.'

I was invited to speak on resilience. Looking back, it was absolutely the right thing to do. It helped many people who were struggling, and I had somehow given them permission to feel what they felt more openly. They could talk about it and let it surface. There was connection and camaraderie.

When I first started, I was doing it more to divert the attention I was getting but when I found the research foundation, my actions gave meaning to what I suffered. It provided me with an opportunity to create a positive impact. That called on courage and compassion for me. I had to give myself room to breathe, to feel what I felt and to be open about it. I went from 'Let's get on with this' to 'Just go with the flow. Allow yourself time and space to feel this. Allow yourself to talk about it. Allow yourself to communicate it with others.'

So that was compassion for myself, but also for others because it enabled them to show that compassion back to me. I think there's some collective wisdom from the experience that other people were privy to; they were part of something else. So, I feel that all three elements came together.

Another aspect of compassion is to receive compassion from others. Often, when we are suffering, our loved ones want to do something for us and often feel helpless to know what to do. So they suffer as a result. If we allow them to show us their compassion through acts of kindness, allowing them to be with us, etc., we are alleviating their suffering too. It's a two-way street. I think Phyllis's story exemplifies this, and Lily also used her experience of breast cancer to help others:

I think when you become more compassionate, it unlocks a lot of the beauty in life, and everything makes sense. I experienced true compassion when I was having treatment for breast cancer. I was diagnosed with breast cancer, and I'd had a double mastectomy. My first round of chemotherapy had made me poorly. At one point I ended up in hospital with neutropenic sepsis and it really frightened me. I did think I might die. The day I got home from hospital I started to lose my hair. So, I had that shaved off. I felt so weak. I could only compare it to feeling like I was a very frail 95-year-old woman.

I was watching a programme, *Loose Women*. Linda Nolan had breast cancer. She was keeping a video diary and they were showing it. I think that was the first time that I felt true compassion. Compassion to me is basically becoming the other person in a way. Hearing her talk, I could feel how I thought she felt. I bawled my eyes out. Sometimes compassion can be confused with empathy or sympathy. It's not that. It goes beyond that. It's about becoming the other person, almost, or the other being – the other living thing; feeling how that person feels. But it's overwhelming.

From then on, I had this overwhelming feeling of compassion. Especially for the people, the ladies that I met along the way, going through breast cancer treatment as well. When you end your chemotherapy, you get to ring a bell to say that you've finished. It still makes me emotional talking about it. That feeling of wanting other people to ring that bell.

I guess my emotional response initially to that programme and then that realisation that we need to feel more for each other made me want to share my own breast cancer story. I wrote a blog. It was cathartic. Writing really helped me. I think because it was coming from a genuine place, warts and all, but with my sense of humour. What I wanted to do was take the fear out of breast cancer for a lot of people. Someone might be able to identify with my story. Even though I knew that Linda would have been so scared, just hearing that somebody else felt the way I felt – had the thoughts that I had – was so reassuring and comforting. And I thought if somebody else takes comfort from something I've written, then that is job done. And it was lovely, such a positive response to my writing. And that's helped me get through that period.

'And how easy was it for you to actually write that blog?' I asked. Lily continued:

So easy because it came from here [the heart]. I wrote it as I would say it. I think the people that know me enjoyed it. It was a way of connecting with people when I felt very disconnected from normal life. At that time, it came naturally because whatever was said needed to be said; it sort of needed to come out of me.

This final example about cancer comes from Ezra, who made the difficult decision to opt for high-risk surgical treatment. The way in which he dealt with himself as well as his family and friends meant that he showed compassion to both himself and others:

The one that sticks in my mind is when I decided to have the operation because it's a high-risk operation. The UK surgeons said I was inoperable. I had to go abroad, which meant being ill in a foreign country, language issues, etc. Also, a high risk of complications, it not working, and potentially my quality of life being worse than when I went in. My decision was very instant, even if I refused to acknowledge that at the start, but it took a lot for me to stay with it in the weeks and months, particularly as the deadline approached.

'So what enabled you to do that?' I wondered.
Ezra explained:

I found it very helpful to talk with leading specialists in the UK and abroad, hearing that taking the 'safe' option was very likely to work out badly in the medium, let alone the longer term.

I got help with the courage from a good friend who gave me a little embroidered Quaker saying, 'Live Adventurously'. I keep that right in front of me. It was a constant reminder for me to choose that option. It's not 'live dangerously', it's 'live adventurously'.

The compassion was not to beat myself up when I panicked and questioned my decision. When people said to me, 'Oh my God, you're not really going to have that done to you?', part of me could have got angry with them because that destabilised me. It is, on one level, a stupid thing to do when you're well, to take such a big risk. So, it meant showing compassion to other people as they interacted with me because they would probably make different decisions for themselves.

It really helped that I've got a supportive partner and very supportive family and friends. They supported my decision once they knew I had thought it through. When I wasn't feeling compassionate to myself there was a lot of compassion coming at me. So that really helped. It works both ways; receiving compassion helps you to have compassion for yourself.

It can be hard to stand up for what you believe is the right thing to do in the face of incredulity. We need to trust our own intuition and listen to what our wisdom is telling us, while showing courage and compassion at the same time. As Ezra said, it is not about being reckless or doing something that is dangerous. There was a deeper knowing on which Ezra based his decision. I am delighted to report that the operation has been successful. In fact, twice, because the cancer recurred.

I heard several accounts of the support that my interviewees gave to ill friends and family. I have shared some examples here. I agree with Kristina – who shares the next story – that we are often moved to acts of compassion when we discover that our friends and loved ones are unwell. We want to help them and alleviate their suffering in any way that we can. Kristina explained:

When you've experienced suffering – say, either you or people close to you have had a major illness, or you've experienced the death of someone close – I think you connect on a human level with people. I think courage, compassion and wisdom is absolutely that: you have that human connection with somebody.

A friend had a brain injury a few years ago. A lot of his friends don't see him anymore and I need a lot of courage to visit him because I find it difficult; his speech and thought processes are not what they used to be, and he is distressed. But I try and connect with him on a human level.

I think at the base level, courage, compassion and wisdom connect human to human. I do display that in this situation, but it's not easy. The easiest thing would be to send a message saying, 'I'm really sorry to hear...' But I think when you are in deep need, people will respond. I respond because I feel it's the right thing to do and I also hope people will respond to me when I'm in deep need.

I feel very sad for him because I know that he knows he's different from how he was; he can remember how he used to be. That's what I find really distressing. He is well cared for and looked after, but his life is now completely different. He wants to do the things he used to do but can't. I feel incredibly lucky that I'm in good health.

Hannah similarly suppressed her emotions to support a friend in need. In this case, Hannah chose to act normally with her friend and did not catastrophise her situation. Sometimes that's what we need, isn't it? We want someone to take us out of ourselves for a while rather than fuss over us, wrap us in cotton wool or share their sadness, fear, grief. Hannah told me:

My very good friend had been out of touch with me at the beginning of this year. I hadn't clicked that there was anything wrong, on a conscious level, but I knew she wasn't in touch. I dropped a few texts. She was busy and that was fine. We finally caught up a week ago. Before Christmas she had been diagnosed with breast cancer. She hadn't wanted to tell anyone other than family.

What did I do that was compassionate? Because I know

her so well, I held back on being shocked, getting caught up with the C-word, or dwelling on what had happened in between then and now. I believed I was being compassionate because I normalised it with her and chatted as we would normally. I acknowledged it in a way that didn't dramatise what had happened. I believe that's how she would have preferred me to behave with her. Sometimes compassion is about doing what's right for the other person. Obviously, my heart and my stomach just fell when she told me, but I actively tried not to show that in my voice or anything because the last thing she needed was for me to be scared.

Emma provides unconditional acceptance of her friend who is struggling with addiction and depression when many of their mutual friends have chosen to stay away. This epitomises the Three Companions for me, and displays a degree of wisdom that we would not typically associate with someone in their twenties:

A friend of mine struggles with drug addiction. That's a big thing in our friendship group because not everyone can cope with that. He is drawn to me because I try not to judge. He has been through a lot in his life, at his young age; he's only 26. When I hear his stories, I am so grateful that I didn't have to go through it at all.

I feel compassion because I want to help him. At times, some of our friends are on the 'You have to go to rehab' train. That's not always the right way for him. I've known him for three years, and he's gone from smoking five joints a day to two a week. I've never pushed him to smoke less because I felt that was what he needed me to be. We have enough friends that encourage him to stop using drugs or smoke less. I felt that he needed someone that was just there and said, 'It's OK. Do what you feel is good. If you think you need it now, do it.' But I also told him that he needed to be careful – 'Because your body doesn't like it if you use a lot of drugs. You're still young, so it's OK. But if you do this for another 20 years, then it's just going to kill you.' We always had open and honest conversations about that, but I never pushed him to stop using.

These last two accounts remind me that we need to tune in to what the other person wants from us. What we intend to be compassionate acts may not be received that way. For example, in the previous story, the narrator took a different approach to others in their group of friends. I could infer that the ones who were telling him to stop using drugs were doing it out of concern for his health and well-being; however, it seems that this was not what he needed. I have personal experience of people close to me who were abusing substances; it is difficult to behave like Emma and be a compassionate presence providing unconditional acceptance and love. It takes a lot of courage and wisdom to be with someone who is an addict and show them compassion rather than judgement.

James showed compassion to a colleague who was having treatment for cancer. She was fearful of the COVID-19 virus and how it impacted both her and her vulnerable daughter. James chose to show his concern and understanding privately, which felt more genuine and personalised to him:

I belong to a group, there are 11 of us and one of us has cancer. So, I'm trying to be supportive of the person who has cancer. Everyone else sends emails to this person and copies everybody in. I try to do it on a one-to-one basis. I think it's more personal.

She's very worried about the virus because having cancer puts her in a very vulnerable position. Her daughter needs a kidney transplant quite urgently and my colleague was going to be the donor but clearly can't be now. So, she's very worried for her daughter. She sent round an anguished text.

Then got a couple of texts, people saying, 'Thinking of you', which is nice. I went back with an email saying, 'I realised it must be very worrying', and, 'We're all here for you and we have to all try and get through this.' So, doing it on an individual basis. She emailed me back and said, 'Thank you for doing that. Thanks for your support. I really appreciate it.'

It can be hard to support our loved ones through courage, compassion and wisdom, as the next stories show. We often have good intentions; however, our own agenda may sometimes get in the way of alleviating the suffering of the person we intend to help. The first story is from Belinda, whose boyfriend was addicted to alcohol. Belinda felt she knew the right path for him and wanted to fight to help him overcome his addiction. Belinda eventually realised that she had to let go of this, which took a lot of courage:

In the time that I lived with my former boyfriend, I thought courage was fighting [for him to stop drinking]. When I look back, I think that giving up this fight could have been a courage moment. To step back or to accept him. So, to give up this aim of 'winning' was courageous.

'What do you mean by you wanted to win – win what?' I wondered. Belinda replied:

My conviction was that: 'If you do it this way, then things will turn out better for you.' So, I thought I had the wisdom that he could change. I think that he knew better than I did that what I wanted for him was no longer possible. So, to accept that, I had to give up my aim. And it was very difficult. Sometimes you have to make a wise decision to turn back and not climb to the end. So, it takes courage sometimes to not fulfil the things you have in your head.

In the next story, Fatima expresses a feeling that is natural to most of us: fear. Her husband had cancer and could not easily be treated where they live in the Balkans. Fatima had faced threats to her life with courage, yet the prospect of losing her husband terrified her:

> When it comes to the health of my husband, I'm so scared. I'm crying all the time. I feel helpless because I have absolutely no control. I can't do anything to make things different or better, or fight. I feel so powerless and I wish I believed in God because it would be easier to look for help, for a decision to be made by someone. That's when I'm not courageous. I don't have that issue with my own health as much as with his health. I had a couple of surgeries and I wasn't really scared that I was going to die. But when it comes to people I love, particularly him, I'm all crazy because my mum died suddenly when I was quite young.

Fatima's fear stemmed from the lack of knowledge and capacity of the medical staff in her country to treat him. An understandable concern. We want our loved ones to be given the best treatment possible, so they have a good prognosis.

Niamh describes her mixed feelings towards her sister. When Niamh's away from her, she can understand that it's frustrating for her sister to see her husband decline. However, when they are together, Niamh feels a degree of irritation with her sister for how she treats her husband. She believes that her sister should accept that she has to shoulder more responsibility for things because that is what Niamh has to do, being a widow. And she does not want to step into the role of making things feel better for her sister. So she's less able to show compassion towards her sister when she's with her:

> I find it hard to be compassionate and do the right thing for my sister, whose husband is suffering from senile dementia. I felt that her anger with him for having it was quite hard to

get alongside. I could understand intellectually. But when I was with her and she was angry with him, saying he should be doing more and he's not trying, I'm trying to say, 'I don't think he can. It's not his fault.' And sometimes witnessing her – she wasn't being unkind to him, but would increase his anxiety. There's a little bit of me that used to say, 'Well, you're saying, he doesn't do this, and he doesn't do that, and you have to do so much more. Join my world – that's what it's like.' I think it could be a more selfish thing; I don't want to feel I've got the responsibility for making it better.

There are many people living with mental health problems. The following examples show how using the Three Companions can make a big difference and help them get back on their feet when they are struggling. Of course, it is not always possible to show these qualities as the latter stories show. But first, though, Saskia's story, which I find to be a moving display of love:

I lived overseas while my kids were small and the three of us moved to the UK about six years ago. My daughter was 12. It was such a hard time for her. It was such a culture shock. She thought she was British; she wasn't. She arrived in Year 8 of school, and it was just like she had dropped from Mars. It was so hard: she found it challenging to fit in and suffered from intense anxiety. She moved school several times and was home-schooled for a while. She couldn't settle and was always worrying. She was constantly dreaming about the next thing and found the present hard to face.

I realised that tough love was what was really needed. I couldn't let her go down. She needed something to tether herself to. My first real act of toughness was to say, 'OK, this is the last school, you're staying here. No matter what it's like, you're just staying. I'll be there with you, but you've got to do this. You have to face things here and now.' It wasn't easy

– she was still absent from school and often all over the place emotionally – but she settled.

I wrote her a letter, which she still has and refers to quite often; she even had it up on her wall for a while. It was a pure love letter to her as a young woman, who I wanted to live in this world rather than an imaginary, 'better' world. Unwittingly, I dug into my deep wisdom to write it: I trusted I knew what she needed and that she was strong enough to take it. She needed some solid ground and some clarity.

I started the letter with an expression of my undying love for her – a love that will never end no matter what she goes through. I let her know that she never need worry about that because it's just there. I think some of my wisdom came through in the force with which I wrote it – all in one go, by hand and in a stream of consciousness. There were no errors; it just came out in one burst. When it was finished, it was finished.

It said, 'This is how life is. These are the tips I have for you to get through it and be present in it. Give yourself time to consider things. Make choices that are good for you, exercise, eat well, choose friends who care about you and share your values.' And it also said, 'This life can be tough, and these are the things you can do to get through it. These are things that will help you have a good life. They're simple, but you need to do them yourself. I can't do them for you, nor can anyone else.'

A few years on, I can see her coming through all of it. She's got a good group of friends. She's an artist; she's doing the stuff that she loves, being courageous and really following her heart. She still has dips, but she's good at managing them. She's become much more resilient. And she's learnt to live firmly in the present as well as have dreams for the future. I take my hat off to her.

And, as I tell this story, I take the hat off to myself as

well. I had the courage to do something that felt risky at the time – being very boundaried and tough in the face of fragile mental health. And it's paid off.

Sofia supported someone with mental health issues to return to work after he had a breakdown. It illustrates how showing compassion to others has a positive impact on ourselves, even if it is not apparent to us and we are unaware of the effect we have had on the other individual:

I have only recently come to understand the impact that this example had on a guy who worked for me. He told this story publicly during Mental Health Week. I had not appreciated at the time, about ten years ago, the impact of what I considered was absolutely doing my job.

He worked for somebody else, had started to struggle with some mental health issues and had been off work for a while. During the period that he was off he came to work for me because there was an organisational restructure. I was aware that he was upset. I didn't know him, so I reached out: 'I know you're off, can we meet? Let's talk about what is going to help to get you back to work. What do you need from me?' He recalled a meeting that we had where he explained his anxieties about returning to work. He said what I did was very simple on one level but was the turning point for the next ten years of his life.

I can remember very clearly, him coming into my office. He was very anxious about coming back to work. I said, 'What is it that you're worried about? What do you think's happening?'

He said, 'Everyone's talking about me.' I made a choice to tell him the brutal truth because the reality was so far off.

I said, 'Actually, no one's talking about it because everyone's really busy. Those people who know you're not here want you to come back. So, if that's your biggest concern, it's not true.'

He then said, 'I'm concerned that I've got 10,000 emails that we haven't made progress on.'

'Just delete them.'

He said, 'But there's work in there and nothing's happening. And they might escalate up to you.'

'Fine, just delete them.' To this day, I can remember saying to him, 'It's not a request, it's an instruction. Delete every single email. When you come back on Monday, we'll just start again.'

In my head, all I did was my job. I wouldn't say it was courageous. I wouldn't say there was great wisdom. I do remember there was compassion. But he said, 'You were pretty brave because you were the only person who bluntly told me, "Actually, no one's talking about you", because everyone else kept patting my arm.'

I sponsor our mental health group in the North West [of England] because I feel strongly about it. This video popped up on Workplace. It was my colleague saying, 'I want to tell you a story about ten years ago.' He told the story and I sat in floods of tears watching it. I don't think I'd understood clearly how difficult it was for him. I had no conception of the impact that it had. Here was someone who's gone on to be an extremely successful person who would have walked out the door.

All I did was the right thing. My job was to help someone who felt vulnerable and unsure come back to work, and have a positive experience. I can remember saying, 'I'm instructing you to do it.' That's very strong; I would usually only say it in a crisis. This wasn't a crisis. But my perception was that here was someone who was struggling with choices and decision making. The most helpful thing I could do was take that decision away from him. Because it's emails. So, from wisdom, it was merely stuff that could be re-created. Relationships can't be re-created. Emails can be rewritten.

I think the interesting thing is that it was only in October of last year that I began to appreciate the impact. My only intent had been to help someone deal with Monday morning.

There must have been something, because, somewhere in my brain, it was logged. So, even though you move on, and ten years of life happen, there must have been something, because when I watched that video, I could tell you exactly the day of the week it was, the time of day, and I can remember the red dress I was wearing.

Sofia did what instinctively felt right. In so doing, she tapped into her Three Companions. If she had intended to have a ten-year impact, it would have been more about her and less about her colleague – and probably not about courage, compassion and wisdom. It's interesting to consider why this meeting, out of the thousands that she has had as a leader, had made such an impression on her.

Sometimes family dynamics interfere with our ability to show courage, compassion and wisdom to our loved ones, as the following stories show. Nadia describes her conflicted feelings towards her sister:

I have a sister, ten years older than me, who's mentally ill, has cancer and is totally isolated. Generally, I just listen to her when we speak on the phone without challenging or contradicting any of her more paranoid beliefs and perceptions of other people's motives. However, at times I feel compelled to challenge her statements, either because her beliefs are affecting her welfare or, on occasion, when I am unable to stop my emotional reactions. In the former situation, I must psych myself to challenge her beliefs and assumptions, aware that she may react angrily and slam the phone down on me. For example, this can be triggered by her refusal of medical treatment for cancer because of fears that doctors may wish to harm her. I'm the only person in her world, therefore it has to be me that does this. There is no one else alive to do so anymore. Is this a kind of courage? Or is it compassion? Or both?

Compassion is a complicated emotion, I find – easy to have in relation to the world and to humankind, but full of tensions about people we are close to. It's interesting because I've not thought about this much before. I feel great compassion for my sister in the abstract and can understand her position and the life events that have caused her mental ill health. But when we speak, it's more difficult to feel this. At this point the irritation and annoyance come to the fore; a familiar emotion as my sister's welfare and needs dominated my childhood and adult life.

Because of the awareness of such conflicting emotions, I have to prepare any time I feel it is vital to challenge her beliefs. I have to think it through and know when I can't manage it emotionally. I do the best I can, trying generally to limit my communications to providing her with a listening, non-critical ear, not challenging her viewpoint and being aware that there are times when I just cannot deal with a situation. It is best, on balance, to maintain communication than risk that I become part of her paranoid beliefs.

This is reminiscent of how Niamh (whom we met earlier) relates to her sister, in that she has compassion for her due to her husband having dementia while she's not with her sister but then finds herself reacting in a different way when they are together. It takes courage to have difficult conversations, knowing that your sister will have an adverse reaction. I also believe that Nadia shows self-compassion and wisdom in recognising when she needs to stop engaging because she does not have the emotional strength at that time.

Leya shares with us another story about the sister she supported by taking care of her finances. The focus of this one is on how she experienced a clash of values with her sister, which then interfered in her ability to show compassion:

I'll go back to my sister, the one that died a couple of weeks ago. I overemphasised courage but not enough compassion. Her death gave me the opportunity to ponder some of that. One of the things that I realised was that I was much better at managing the situation – at fulfilling my responsibility with a capital 'R', and managing with a capital 'M'. I was much less concerned about being compassionate or kind. I realised that there were many opportunities over the course of those 12 years where I could have done a much better job of being kind. I treated her more like a burden and a responsibility and less like a sister.

It is not something of which I'm proud. The day after I heard she'd died, I was almost catatonic with this very deep sense of my own grief. Not my grief that she was dead, because I believe in an afterlife and that she's better off. The grief was that I had not been true to myself in the way that I had dealt with her. That I expressed this leadership philosophy – of being kind to people, of showing compassion, of really considering the individual – and I did not treat her that way.

I'm sorry I didn't confront it sooner. That I didn't sit down and think that through in a more mindful way, years ago. My daughter reminded me: 'For the last 12 years you have done what no one else in the family could do. You are the manager in the family. You are the executive, and you did what nobody else was willing to take on. Maybe that was your job. Maybe your job was to help find the one who could be kind. Maybe you can't do everything.' She was very compassionate to me. That reframing helped me, and it was very wise. But in all honesty, I don't think it took me off the hook because being integral with myself, I could have been kinder during that 12-year period.

I asked, 'And in your reflection, have you got insights as to what stopped you?'

Leya replied:

Can I be entirely candid with you? I resented that she was making no effort to take care of herself, was essentially manipulating the family. I have this very deep-seated appreciation of personal responsibility. So, every one of my interactions with her violated that from her side because she was not accepting personal responsibility. Every time I interacted with her, it grated on me. I felt, whatever she could do, she should have been doing, instead of this learnt helplessness she adopted in order to have somebody else take care of her. I didn't have enough mental and emotional strength to pull out of that and give to her freely, without any strings attached. I was so wrapped up in the 'There are so many of these things you should be doing for yourself.'

Leya expressed regret that she was unable to confront her feelings earlier and change her behaviour towards her sister. It's at times like these that I think we need to show self-compassion and learn from our experiences. We are not perfect; we are human beings who make mistakes or behave in ways that, at times, are less than ideal. That's natural and normal. If we can harness self-compassion when we are feeling bad about ourselves, this will increase our resilience and ability to show more empathy in the future. We will look at this in more detail in Part Three.

The next story shows a different aspect of how established patterns of behaviour can hinder us from showing compassion. We meet Hannah again as she describes the difficulty she had in changing the dynamic in her relationship with her mother. In her case, it was about expressing her love in hugs:

A situation where I regret not being more compassionate was with my mother, who was in a care home, because she had dementia and cancer.

There were staff in that care home who were more compassionate than me – that expression of compassion through physical touch. They were more loving and hugged her more than I did. Dementia is a very difficult thing to deal with. I saw other people giving that to my mother. They were strangers who decided that they loved my mum and would give her a hug.

Sometimes, I think the roles we have in life present enormous barriers to our ability to deliver compassion. I think there is something about the relationship that either allows you to be compassionate or is a boundary or barrier that's almost insurmountable. My mum and I did love one another. We would give one another a hug and a kiss, but we weren't an overly touchy family. I was never able to change that behaviour, even though my mother needed it. I would give more physical compassion, more patient compassion to anyone else, more than I could give to my mother.

I know at an intellectual level that the biggest hurdle is to move from being the child to the adult when your parents have dementia. You must become the adult in the situation because they're regressing. You must start making decisions and behaving in a different way. You'd give a child a lot of hugs if they needed it, but I couldn't break that habit of a lifetime. I could in all other aspects of caring for her. I would fight tooth and nail to make sure she had the right care, make sure everything worked. But that one thing of the physicality of it, I didn't do very well. I could behave in a compassionate way with another lady that was there, touch and hug her much more easily than I could my mother.

In talking with many people, I discovered that it is often harder to show compassion to those closest to us because of the shared history of the relationship and the dynamics that have been created between us. In these instances, we do need to be more intentional about how we

85

show compassion, rather than react or behave as we have always done to different stimuli. Not at all easy to do!

Henry saw that one of his colleagues was struggling with some mental health issues. He wanted to help her. Unfortunately, his well-intentioned intervention did not have the desired impact:

A colleague on the same management team as me was really struggling with her work. I became very aware that she was subject to mood swings and odd behaviours. I went to see a colleague of mine, the three of us were peers, and said, 'I reckon this is going on with Karen and I'm going to talk to our boss.'

Tim said, 'Whatever you do, don't go there. Don't do it.'

I said, 'Why not?'

He said, 'Trust me. Don't go there. Incendiary. It'll be a disaster. Don't do it.'

I said, 'I've got to do it. Karen's really struggling and our boss doesn't know. I've got to go and tell.'

I went to my boss and told him. And I had the most difficult conversation I've ever had in my management career. He heard me out and then said, 'From this point on, I'm always going to act with you as if this conversation has never happened. Is there anything else you'd like to talk about today?'

I did not know what to do. I still look back on that exchange and think, 'God that was a horrible piece of management behaviour from him towards me. And a horrible piece towards Karen.' I look back on that and think, 'Tim gave me some wisdom based on some knowledge that he obviously had about the situation, our boss, my temperament. He was advising me, "Don't do it." I ignored the wise advice, went in anyway and damaged my relationship with my boss and my effectiveness, psychologically, for a long time. I don't think it helped Karen at all because of a lack of wisdom. The situation didn't work out at all well.

It can be hard to balance trusting our intuition with the advice that someone gives us. That said, I know that I have a different issue, which is to blindly trust advice I receive from people whom I respect. In both situations, I think it's a good opportunity to harness our curiosity and ask why the individual is giving us that counsel.

The final moments of someone's life

I have not witnessed the final moments of someone's life. When my dear uncle, who lived in Sweden, was close to death, my husband and I went to spend a few days with him, his wife and my cousins. We had chosen a gift for him and his wife that expressed the love we felt for him. I was delighted that he still had the strength to open and appreciate it. He died less than two weeks later.

Similarly, I received a call from Javier to tell me that his mother was close to death in a hospice. (Javier told us about a meaningful moment for him with his dying mother on page 52.) In that instance, my new husband and I flew to London to be with her, Javier and my friend's older sister. It was ten days after we had got married. She had been too ill to make the journey, so I was able to share a little of our wedding day with her. She died four days later.

In both situations, I was so happy to spend time with these people before they died and to offer compassion to their families through my presence. I think in these circumstances my courage lay in facing their death, while wisdom lay in knowing that I needed to see them and convey my love one more time.

When we are not with someone when they die, I think it is easy to feel guilty, particularly if there are societal or familial expectations that we should be there. This is often true for parents, siblings, partners and children. I had this experience when my second husband died in February 2020. It was a complicated situation due to his alcoholism;

we had recently separated. I spent time with him when he was in hospital, not knowing it was the last time I would see him alive. We had some tender moments during that visit. And I'm glad we were able to declare our love for each other. The following night I had an experience in which I told him, 'It's OK, you can go now.' He died two days later.

I felt bad about not being present when he died even though we were separated. This was heightened because his ex-wife was there. I have had to exercise significant self-compassion to be at peace with that. Also, to have had the courage to unpick the story that I am telling myself about this and the wisdom to recognise that I had done all that I could for him – and that was enough.

Often the distress we feel at the passing of a loved one from life to death makes it hard to access the Three Companions. During the interviews, I heard a number of stories about the demise of parents, spouses, close friends and relatives. Some of these were about confronting mortality and others were about supporting others in their loss.

The first story depicts how Eleni was able to employ the Three Companions in her dealings with her brother in the period leading up to their mother's death, yet she did not have that capacity at other times due to empathy overload:

> Towards the end of my mum's life, and then the last days when we were around her bed, was when all Three Companions came together. I don't know if it was the realisation that this truly was it.
>
> What stands out was talking my brother through things. I think, because of his emotional response to it, he turned into a bit of an idiot over the week that we were in the hospital. His energy and the things he was doing were random. Within minutes of my mum dying, he looked at his watch and said, 'Do you think that we can get back to Scotland?' That's not what he meant. I understand now. I think through that process I tried to give him some wisdom, but I wasn't

very good at it because I just got really peed off with him. So, it was a lack of compassion and wisdom.

We did a lot of talking. There were all sorts of things going on for him, which I've now learnt about. To me, he was an absent sibling who had a lot going on. So, I think it was about the wisdom to allow him the space to talk that through and explain what was happening, without interruption, without judgement. And that was wisdom for me because I hadn't done that before; I'd made assumptions.

I asked, 'So, what got in the way of you being able to show that compassion?'

'I got too involved in myself,' Eleni said. 'I'd been the primary carer and I was looking at how things were affecting me.'

'Being aware that taking on someone else's suffering incapacitates us, and having boundaries to determine how much you let in, can help,' I said. 'How do those resonate with what you went through?'

Eleni continued:

They do resonate. To add to that, often when we consider compassion, our automatic response is to think about other people, but we forget about compassion for ourselves. Sometimes we are going through so much. I used to say to my brother, 'I've just got empathy burnout here. I'm just not feeling anything.' So, compassion can be about us as well.

Louise talked with me about being seen as difficult by her siblings because she didn't join the bedside vigil when her father was dying. She had provided support to her parents in the five months from when he was diagnosed with cancer of the oesophagus until he died. Her running to and fro was tinged with guilt at not being there when something happened to him, such as a fall, and recognising that she had her own life to live. She was supporting her son and his wife in addition to her parents. She explained:

91

When Dad went into the hospice, he actually lasted ten days, which nobody thought he would, bless him. I rang my sister to tell her, and she said, 'I'm coming tomorrow. My employer has told me I can take as much time as I like. I'm staying to the end.' I thought, 'Fine, I'll get the hell out of it.' My sister had to go for two or three days, so my husband and I went back to cover her for that time.

She came back, and my brother appeared out of nowhere, having not visited Dad at all during his illness. He and his wife decided with my sister that they would do the bedside vigil. I said, 'I won't join you in that. I will come back as soon as Dad's died and deal with all the post-death stuff.'

This worked well but I felt something from them about the fact I wasn't there by his bedside. My mother was there as well, which I think was difficult for her. I would have given her the choice of whether she wanted to be there 24 hours a day. I think she'd have said, 'No', because she's got a good sense of self-preservation. They assumed that she would do what they were intending to do. In the end, it got to the point where they were all desperate. I agreed that on the Friday, if Dad hadn't died, we were going to go up to the hospice and take over for 24 hours while they went off to get some sleep. In fact, he died at five o'clock on the Friday morning. So we didn't have to do it.

There was this big thing about being there at the actual moment of death, even though he'd been unconscious for several days. There was wisdom there because sometimes you don't have to be there. I'd said goodbye to him the previous weekend when he was still aware I was saying goodbye. He died on Friday. I turned up on the Sunday and spent a week doing all the stuff, the death certificate, getting his belongings from the hospice etc., that needed doing. And suddenly, my siblings were gone. I think wisdom was being very practical: if we all crowd round his deathbed, then almost by definition, we leave Mum on her own afterwards because we've also got lives to get on with.

I think the Three Companions came together because it would have taken Louise's compassion for her mother and inner strength and courage to withstand the subtle pressure from her siblings.

Elaine also talked to me about her father dying, and how she and her sisters went home to be with their parents in his final hours. She highlights the potential beauty in witnessing someone's death if we are to see this as a passage to a different place:

When my father died, I was with him. That took quite a lot of courage. That was quite scary. When somebody is dying, they go on a very intimate and personal journey, and you go with them. Now I have that inner wisdom, inner experience. Being with somebody at the end of their life brings everything – compassion, courage – into sharp focus. It was a very moving, introspective time.

He had a stroke. Five months later, eight weeks after his initial diagnosis, he died. We all went home to my mum, and stayed with him, particularly when we saw that he was going to die within hours. We were with him throughout. When my mum died, we did the same. You help somebody's passing. I think that was a personal experience where I had to call on all sorts of things.

The next story also highlights that we can develop more compassion for individuals when we have been through a time of suffering ourselves. George witnessed the suffering of his wife as she died of cancer, and the impact it had on his sons and himself. Having been through this experience, he could connect more deeply with the needs of others:

I think that the compassionate side of things has grown in strength. When my wife had cancer, 13 or 14 years ago, and subsequently died three years ago, I learnt significantly from

93

that. I learnt not to judge people as to how they were behaving or responding to these things. Also, to feel compassion for other people who had difficulties that they were trying to deal with and allow them to talk about some of those things. I've become much more generous with my compassion since that time. I'm much quicker to spot those sorts of things and offer, 'Do you want to talk about that? You can get in touch with me.' Or, 'I've got a friend, he had a similar thing, maybe I could put you in touch with him. You could have a chat about that.' Those sorts of things became much easier.

I asked, 'What had changed for you that enabled you to do that more?' George explained:

I suppose, trauma. You've only got one life. When you're closely involved in an experience where that happens, it becomes far more real than a catchphrase. Then you realise, 'If I can sit down with somebody, share my experience, and make their life half an hour easier, or make it two hours or three weeks better, that's a success.'

Individuals who come through a traumatic time often want to help others. We saw that earlier with Phyllis and Lily. If we can see life's struggles as gifts and moments for us to grow, this helps to build our resilience and ability to deal with challenges.

Earlier, Niamh gave us insight into the source of her irritation with her sister, explaining that she had to forge a new life for herself after her husband and partner for 30 years died. She did this not only for herself but also for her son. Sometimes Niamh had to call on her Three Companions to keep pushing through when she would have preferred to curl up in a ball and let the world go by. She elaborated:

My husband died nine years ago. I think that it takes courage to find a new life. Overall, we had a good relationship. It was an honest relationship. It was robust. Having been with somebody since I was 20, to forge a life that was ultimately on my own, it's not terribly brave; people do it all the time, but sometimes it would have been easier to curl up and not do things. I felt, from my son's point of view, I needed to be my own person and be an independent person, so that he didn't feel burdened by my grief.

I recognise the urge to curl up and not do anything. After I separated from my first husband, when I was alone at home, I felt lonely and wanted the time to pass quickly. When I moved out of the marital home, I found an apartment within five minutes' walking distance so that my children could spend weekends with me and go easily between the two places. On the weekends that I did not have my children to stay, I often curled up on the sofa and slept. I realise now that I was drawing on my Three Companions at the time to keep strong because I knew that separating was the right thing to do.

Some of my interviewees shared with me their regret at not being there for a close friend who was either dying or grieving for the loss of a loved one. Idris tells us that he struggles to process news about illness or death. He recognises that there is something profound going on for him and he is not yet ready to face it:

I know that if there's death around me or something that's quite profound like that, I struggle to figure out what to do with that information or even how to connect with other people. It does something deep for me in a way that I haven't figured out how to process. I don't know where it comes from.

The first time I became aware of it was probably in my twenties. A close friend of mine, his sister died. I was quite close to the family. The funeral came around and I could not bring myself to go. I couldn't be there for whatever reason.

The fact that I'm telling this story, 30 years later – it still sticks with me. It's one of my very few regrets in life. I regret not being there to support him, his brother and the family. That's when I knew there was something there. I don't know if it's a protection or if it's a fear. I'm not quite sure what it is, partly because I try not to. I'm not ready to explore it too much. So, I don't think about it much. I know that thing is there. I'll just leave it over there for a while. I'll deal with it some other time, but not now.

I wonder if it is his own fear, or the inherited fear from previous generations? Idris will need courage to exercise self-compassion and do the healing that seems to be required.

Let's meet Saskia again. In this story, she tells us about her fear of facing death when her friend was diagnosed with cancer. Since then, she has learnt to be present and hold a space for others in their grief, as she goes on to share:

This is a really big one for me. I'll probably cry my eyes out as it's one of my biggest regrets. But I learnt from it, so I'll tell you that bit too.

When I was in my early twenties, I went travelling and met a lovely young man and kindred spirit – full of healthy vitality and energy. We had an intense friendship and then kept loosely in touch when we returned home. A couple of years later, I heard he had liver cancer in his mid-twenties. I was so scared to see him sick that I never went to see him before he died. Oh, my goodness, it still brings up emotion in me. It's one of the biggest regrets of my life – that I was not brave enough to go and see him. I didn't have the courage to do that. I know it would have meant a huge amount to him and I didn't show up.

My cousin died about six years ago now. I was living overseas at the time. We hadn't seen a lot of each other, but I'd always felt a connection with him. He'd been living with a debilitating genetic condition for many years. Then I heard from my dad that he was dying, and it was a matter of weeks. I had a real visceral sense that 'now's the time'. So, I came back to the UK and went to see him. I said goodbye to him and faced illness and death. We had the most beautiful and straightforward conversation. I asked him what it was like and what advice he had for me. I was able to tell him how much I loved him. I did all those things that I didn't do with my friend. I cried throughout it all and I let that be OK. And for the whole weekend, my uncle – my cousin's father – hosted me and held me with love, at the same time as he was witnessing his son die. His dignity, compassion, and generosity in the face of heartbreak also left a lasting impression on me.

I think that saying goodbye to my cousin was one of the best, wisest, most courageous and compassionate things I have ever done. I did something similar for my dad a couple of months later when he was in a coma. I travelled across Europe to sit with him and stroke his arm and tell him how much I loved him. He didn't remember when he woke up, but that didn't matter. I did the right thing.

The courage to face my fear around illness and death has triggered a deep interest in grief and sorrow. I have even trained as an end-of-life doula. In the end, the pain of not having honoured my friend as he died propelled me into a very different and much wiser place.

Sometimes we are not able to show compassion for others because we are coping with our own suffering. Manon's partner had been diagnosed with terminal cancer. During this distressing time, the mother of Manon's close friend died. While Manon felt that she could have been more compassionate towards her friend at the time, she realised in the retelling of the story that she was dealing with her own grief, which limited her capacity. It was a time for self-compassion, as she describes:

A friend lost her mother a couple of years ago. When her mother died, looking back, I don't I think I was as compassionate as I could have been. I made too many assumptions. I knew my friend had a difficult childhood and assumed that my friend was quietly relieved when her mother died of old age.

I lost my partner three years ago to cancer. It was probably about a year after my friend lost her mother. Some people were compassionate to me, and I appreciated so much those people around me who really cared. That made me reflect on whether I'd been compassionate and caring enough to someone I class as a very good friend. It wasn't as if it wasn't acknowledged, or I wasn't there for her. Maybe it's that I was going through my stuff. My partner had terminal cancer at the time that her mother died. I had forgotten about that. On reflection, I just thought I wasn't there enough for her, but I think I had my head wrapped around other stuff.

Amanda lost a dear friend to motor neuron disease. She is a healer and used her gifts to help him in his passage to death. And she employed her Three Companions to alleviate the suffering of his wife in a way that she could accept:

My friend had motor neurone disease. When he got it, I thought, 'I'm going to use my spiritual gifts.' I went round and said, 'Please allow me to work with you.' And he did. He asked me very early on if I would do his funeral. With motor neuron disease, you lose everything. Your mind can function, and you cannot move a thing. It's a horrid disease. I worked with him to be comfortable with dying.

I also had to be compassionate with his wife. I had to use a lot of compassion at that time. Because I can see what's going on for him – you're looking at someone who, in the end, couldn't go to the toilet for himself, he couldn't do anything, he could just grunt.

We were very lucky to be there when he died. I was able to see over his spirit. That took a lot of courage because I had to go in there, in a way, push my way in. I didn't have to push very hard; they're my friends. But I had to use a lot of compassion because you had to be so careful what you said. At the same time, he wanted you to be normal.

'How did you show compassion to his wife?' I wondered. Amanda replied:

By being there. It was like reaching a brick wall because she would just clam up. I'd say, 'Let me do some healing.'

'No, my husband needs it, I don't,' she'd say.

She's always listened to my husband. In the days before my friend had a carer, I would go in, do the healing, and do the bits that I needed to with him. His wife took it as her opportunity to go out with my husband. They'd walk the dog. Then my husband would say what needed to be said in his own way. And she would listen.

One thing that's always quite difficult for me, because when you're short, people around you are taller. You're almost like a child. So you can't just put your arms around someone. So people say, 'You don't hug a lot.'

I say, 'Well, there're two reasons: first, because I had cancer and I got every germ going. Second, it is very difficult unless people are sitting down.'

With my friend, I did hands on healing with him, which was to make him feel better, not to cure him. But also, to ease his passage, about feeling comfortable about leaving this world.

I think the other side of it was the human side of losing your friend. I used to go home, and sometimes cry, driving round the M25 because that was my release. I totally got the whole journey and understood that it was all OK because I think life goes on. But I still had to have that human physical release.

It must have been a poignant time for Amanda, knowing that she was helping her friend and his wife through their suffering, and coping with her own loss and grief.

The following two stories are examples of people supporting sisters who'd lost a loved one. In the first account, Maeve rushed to support her sister after the suicide of her nephew. She did not think about her own grief or needs and focused on being strong for her sister:

> When my sister lost her son last year, I went into overdrive with being very courageous. I had to be the strong person. I think that's why I suddenly hit rock bottom at the other end. It wasn't really me. I literally took on this armour. I needed to be strong for them. I couldn't show too much emotion. I needed to be very thoughtful and kind to them. As soon as it all happened, I rushed up to be with them. After the funeral, I took time to be with my sister, trying to ease everything, I suppose, and wanting to be there for her.

Denise also went to be by her sister's side. Her sister's husband was in hospital and eventually died. Like Maeve, Denise submerged her own grief to be strong for her sister. She only allowed herself to release some of her sorrow when she was alone again:

> When my sister's husband died, I was at her house. He'd gone into hospital for an emergency operation the day before Christmas Eve. He was getting better but then he got an infection and was moved into a specialist intensive care unit. This was Christmas 2016. On New Year's Eve, I was planning to meet people for drinks, and I suddenly thought, 'Why am I doing this? My sister can't be having much of a New Year's Eve.'
> She had been sitting by a hospital bed for a week with a

guy who had gone into a coma. It was awful. I remember going over on New Year's Day. She'd been married just over a year before that. My niece, Rosie, had never rolled out the welcome mat for him and was feeling guilty. So, my sister was stressed and I'm trying to manage them both. His two sons turned up and they were crying. I'm hugging these boys and I don't really hug people.

I'm trying to be brave because the consultant had given me a list of what they had given him. We went back in the evening. I'm trying not to panic. I'm trying not to admit that I'm feeling anything. I think the overriding thing there was compassion for everybody. When we went in the evening, the consultant gave us a phone number. He said, 'This is for just his bed, not the ward. It's an intensive care unit; if they're not busy, they'll answer.' And he said, 'You can come and go as you please, tonight. Just buzz to get in.'

I thought, 'When you're told you can come and go as you please, and you've got a number for his bed, it's not good. If it wasn't New Year's Day, I know what they'd be telling us.'

The next morning, they asked, 'How long will it take to get everybody here? We need to switch the machines off.' I think that's one of the hardest things; it hurt. It was awful seeing my sister lose her husband. And seeing his sons and their mother. They switched off the machines and now we're just waiting for when we could call time of death.

I think when that was over, we went for a walk in the park and talked about the practical things that needed to be done. I realised it was the second of January, and the next day, I was supposed to go back to work. I was doing contracting at the time, so if I didn't work, I didn't get paid. I said, 'Do you mind if I drive back home, pick up my laptop and bring it back? Then I can work from yours?'

And she said, 'I don't want you to drive there and back in a day.' She didn't want me out of her sight.

I said, 'You're quite right. You know what, I won't work.'

I dealt with everything on autopilot. I think that was a compassion overdrive. I spent four nights sleeping on the sofa. I had not had a minute to myself, and I needed my own space. When I got in the car to go home, all I thought was, 'I don't know if I can drive.' Because it didn't hit me until that moment. I'll never forget that journey because I really had to force myself to concentrate. I don't think I ever did grieve properly, because it still affects me far more than I ever expected it would. And I just think that sometimes your compassion is needed so much that you forget what you need.

I have noticed that we often tend to the needs of others at our own expense. We don't take care of ourselves. However, it is no good if we do that and then collapse ourselves, as Maeve did. Research shows that exercising self-compassion allows us to show more compassion and empathy to others.[11] While it can feel selfish and indulgent to focus on our emotions and needs, exercising self-compassion increases our capacity to be with and support others. We will look at this in Part Three, but first, let's turn our attention to the Three Companions in other situations.

Parenting

As parents, we have an enormous responsibility to take care of our children and bring them up to the best of our ability. We know that the way we parent has a significant impact on our children. Whether by commission or omission, we teach them life lessons (positive and negative) that they can carry with them into adulthood. Being intentional about using our Three Companions can help us navigate this demanding and precarious path in a way that supports the growth of our children and ourselves.

Creating the conditions for our children to fully experience life and what they are capable of is, in my opinion, one of the greatest gifts we can give them. Recognising and responding to their unique needs, rather than our hopes and fears, is not always easy to do. I think it is important to notice what is happening within us in each moment, whether that is joy, excitement and pride, or we are triggered and feel irritated, annoyed or frustrated. We can then be curious about the underlying meaning of these emotions and what purpose they are serving us.

I didn't have this reflective practice when my children were young. I responded to their needs and showed empathy as much as was possible for me at that time. It is only in the last few years that I have explored my feelings towards them and tried to change my behaviour. They are 27 and 29 now; it's never too late!

In this chapter, we will hear tales of individuals who did or did not use the Three Companions in some parenting situations. While we may not all be parents, we are someone's child. So there are lessons that we can deduct from these stories, even if we have no children of our own.

Let's begin with Niamh, who shows great courage, compassion, and wisdom in nurturing her son:

My eldest son died when he was ten weeks old. I think that there is nothing quite like losing a child. It's 41, 42 years ago, and you can still see that when I think about it. My husband and I knew we wanted to be parents even though we couldn't parent our eldest. So, we had another child; that's my son who's now 41. He nearly died at six weeks of age. He contracted septicaemia and meningitis. We didn't know whether he would live or die. And we didn't know when, finally, he was on the mend what that would mean for him. Nor could the consultant tell us because he had never known a baby who had been as ill as my son and survived.

It was something that we had to live with and make the right decisions for him. He developed epilepsy when he was 11, a big after-effect. Although they said he would probably not be sporty, he was a brilliant swimmer, and he rode. With the epilepsy, I was courageous because it would have been easy to curtail his life. He did triathlons and I had nightmares about him being out on a racing bike, practising on the road.

Both my husband and I were very clear that the epilepsy must not define him. He must be allowed to be himself and do what he wants to do. I was supported in that decision by his neurologist, who said the only thing he should not do was parachute jumping. So, I think that was an ongoing kind of courage. It was fuelled by wanting the best for him and putting his needs and what was right for him beyond what would have felt safer for me.

We return next to Gloria. After her mother's death, at the tender age of 12 she stepped into the role of taking care of her brothers and sisters. Today, she is in her eighties and still the matriarch of her family:

I collected my brothers and sisters, who were being abused by aunts and uncles. When I took them back to the house, there was no way of knowing how we would buy meat or anything, but I felt, as the eldest, much was expected of me. I couldn't bear to see them suffering. I felt it was far better for us to be together. I thought I could better guide them; make sure that they had morning prayers and clean clothes, and would go to school. I didn't know if I could do it. I supposed I would do what my mother would have done.

I think we can see that, in addition to the compassion she clearly felt for her siblings, Gloria demonstrated courage by assuming the mother role at such a young age. It seems that her innate wisdom guided her that this was the best path for them all.

A familiar situation that parents often face is ensuring that our children get the right level of education for them. It is tough making a decision that balances their immediate happiness with providing for their future. Samuel describes the process he and his wife went through when they felt that their son was insufficiently stretched at school to match his abilities:

My youngest son was happy at a state school, but also very bright. The school was struggling to teach him to his level. He had an incredibly good group of friends, many of whom he had grown up with. This was a big concern because, to me and my wife, it was clear he was at the wrong school.

We were taking a risk with his education and his happiness. We had to think through how to support our son with the decision and move because it wouldn't lead to the right outcome if our son didn't feel supported and looked after. I think we got the balance right because he ultimately went to the different school and did very well there. He has moved on to high school in a much better situation than if he hadn't.

I asked, 'So, can you tell me a little bit more about what you did?' and Samuel told me:

The most compassionate piece was not to give him the choice about doing a taster day at the school. This required no commitment to change school. We then gave him the option of whether to go there or not once he'd had that day. We tried to get the balance right – between giving him the facts and his feelings – to make a more informed decision.

We did a lot of work to make sure that it wouldn't impact his social relationships. We invested a lot of time speaking to parents of children who were at his previous school. We had various parties and things to try and maintain that. We made sure that we invested in the social relationships so that piece wasn't impacted, he wasn't losing something to gain something else.

'And how did he respond?'
Samuel continued:

He was adamant he wasn't going to the taster day. He was unbelievably upset that we'd even suggested the idea, let alone booked it. He ultimately went because we said, 'You can have the choice afterwards.' He came away from the day beaming, 'Wow, amazing school and all the opportunities! And these are the things that they do that I've never done before...' So, he came around to it quite quickly.

You make the decision but then you've got the summer holiday before the new academic year starts. He was up and down through that period and needed a lot of reassurance about it. Once he got going with it, he realised it was the right thing to do. So, it's getting through that classic change curve.[12]

We genuinely felt it was the right thing to do and felt a sense of responsibility to do it. We saw it as being compassionate in pushing him down that route. We also knew that once he got there, it would be fine.

Finn's story illustrates how hard it can be to act compassionately in a way that resonates for others because we need to also tune in to what is going on for us:

My feeling is that I act out of self-interest much more than I act out of the interests of others, either by retiring into myself and therefore not being available to be compassionate, or by being a bit slow on the uptake when there's an opportunity to be compassionate. And realising too little too late or getting it wrong. The most obvious recent examples of that would be trying to behave in a sensitive way to my daughter and just be compassionate. She suffers from levels of anxiety requiring treatment with palliative drugs. And she's hypersensitive, particularly if she picks up there is non-genuineness in the room. So, I'm trying to be a genuine dad and trying also to find out ways in which someone like this could be helped. And then being fearful of getting it wrong because the consequence of getting it wrong is that you get your head torn off.

When he gets it wrong, Finn reflects honestly and courageously, in my opinion, to understand why:

I like to feel that what I do is effective. And I give myself a hard time when I've got it wrong for somebody. When I've tried to hold out a hand to somebody, for a start I let them know that I'm resonating with and listening to what they're saying – that I 'get' it, and I offer a consequent thought that they might find helpful – but you don't know how it's going to land with the other person. But afterwards the hard time

I give myself sounds like: 'I really fucked that one up.' And then I do some work to figure out: in what way did I make a mess in that situation? If it's my daughter, she'll tell me directly the ways in which I made a mess. That's quite helpful to know; that's how it happened. But I've lost count of the number of people where, through emotional carelessness, what started out as a desire to be helpful and compassionate has just gone wrong.

Finn genuinely wants to do what is right for others without being intrusive or insistent, which is what makes his behaviour compassionate and wise in my eyes. He shows this in his desire to support his son:

I know that Simon's greatly in need. He and I have not done the preparatory work necessary to enable some of these difficult conversations where I can get him to face what he is under the cosh about. He needs his dad to just be his dad about it and not try and do the psychotherapy thing. You must do some preparatory work to enable that to take place. You might call that wisdom, to be able to stand off that.'

As parents we are often tested, particularly when our children do not behave in ways that we want them to. That is particularly true when we are out in public and feel the eyes of the world judging us, as these next two examples illustrate. Cameron told me:

My oldest daughter was challenging when she was younger. She was often very angry even when she was quite small. I could see that she was very anxious and there'd be times where she'd be kicking off in public to the point where people were watching, 'What's going on?' Literally coming up and saying there's something wrong with your child. It was difficult at times. We wondered if she might have some autistic tendencies because of this 'I can't cope with change' or 'I can't cope with noise' or 'I can't cope with things that are not going the way that I want so I get absolutely insanely angry.'

Cameron went on to explain how he and his wife were able to show courage, compassion, and wisdom towards their daughter:

We didn't get it right all the time because sometimes you had a bad day or were impatient. But as much as we could, our approach was about, 'What do you need? What's going on for you?' You're trying to understand what was going on. Praising her for when she did go out and was 'calm', but I knew that was often a real stretch for her. Being able to have those conversations. Being able to say to her, 'What are the choices you need to make? What went well for you? How do you need to organise your life so that you have it the way that you want?' Recognising that she was prone to anxiety but not to label her as an 'anxious person'. Helping her to recognise that it was OK for her to need a lot of time by herself to recharge her batteries, that she might be more 'introverted' than a lot of other people and being OK with that. Working hard to say, 'That's all right', and encouraging her to do things she wanted to do and not feel bad about that. That's taken courage, compassion and wisdom over a long period of time.

By focusing on their daughter's needs rather than how they felt the world was judging them, Cameron and his wife were able to give her the support that she needed to be herself. This reminds me of Saskia's letter to her daughter, which we looked at earlier. Saskia tuned in to her needs and gave her daughter some lessons to cope with her life.

In contrast, when I asked Milly, 'Can you think of an instance where you feel that you could have shown courage or compassion – and when you haven't?' she ascribed her inability to use the Three Companions to a concern for social norms and a fear that her children may turn out to be ill-mannered adults:

> I think in bringing up children, it comes up almost every day – when they're being absolutely infuriating and rude. I'm overly influenced in my first reactions by a concern about social norms and what other people would think, like being in a restaurant and my children are being irritating. There would be times when I would react out of fear of what kind of people they might turn out to be if they didn't understand how to behave properly. And then taking two steps back and thinking, 'Hang on, this is a 13-year-old.'
>
> I very much believe that happy children don't behave badly. It doesn't mean you forgive any kind of crap that they come out with. But to take two steps back and think, 'Get over your fear that you've failed in some way because they are misbehaving, or they've been rude or argumentative or defiant.' I think, 'Hang on a sec, the child is telling me something by his bad behaviour. He's telling me something's bothering him. These are still innately good people. They haven't gone out and messed up in the world.'

Like Cameron, pondering the underlying reason for her child's behaviour enabled Milly to reframe the situation and let go of her irritation.

Phyllis feels a lot of pressure to perform on all fronts – at work and home, and as a mother and businesswoman. In the heat of the moment, she can get frustrated with her kids. Like Milly, when she calms down, she sees that she needs to respond rather than react and show them compassion:

> Let me share an example of my not being courageous and compassionate with my kids. Sometimes, I feel compartmentalised. People see one side of me, but my

family sees a different side. Perhaps, with family, you feel more secure and so you are more relaxed. I can become very short-tempered with my kids, and I don't always give them the time of day. I don't always allow them a voice. I care about them a lot; I value their opinion greatly and have conversations with them all the time. But I also feel pressured. There are so many things going on, so much that needs to be accomplished. I've got my own business and we moved to Canberra three years ago, so there are a few things going on. Of course, there's pressure with work, school and raising a family of young kids. Those pressures create tension.

I often treat my kids as if they are adults, expecting them to understand, to regulate, to do as adults would do. I know I have high expectations and when things do not happen as they should, I get upset. I scream and shout. I also have out-of-body experiences where I can see myself going absolutely crazy. I talk to myself: 'You need to get a grip. You're not dealing with this situation appropriately. You are reacting, not responding.' I regret my actions and try to start over. I always want to undo what I've done.

I know I need to be more compassionate when it comes to the kids. I know I need not be as hard on them as I am and to pause and reflect a lot more. I need to show more compassion and understanding to see it from their perspective because they will often say, 'No, that's not what I was trying to do.' When calmer, you realise that they are indeed telling the truth.

Camila told me how she utilised the Three Companions to handle a tricky situation that developed between her daughter and her niece, who were living with her during the first lockdown of the COVID-19 pandemic. Unsurprisingly, being cooped up led to some tensions during an otherwise harmonious time for all three. We often feel that we need to act to resolve a dispute. Here Camila took the brave decision not to step in, while also acknowledging how her daughter felt:

> [My everyday acts of courage were] mostly around two young women cooped up and knowing, when there's a flashpoint, whether to act or to bide your time. I think one was irritating the other. My daughter wants me to act and is slightly frustrated that I'm not having a household meeting. I'm thinking that will make things worse, but I don't want to say that because I want to value her judgement. So, the courage for me was to let that all pour out, listen to it, agree enough to not devalue someone and to recognise it was not something I wanted to fix. She said she would deal with it head on if I didn't. I had to have the courage to believe that if that happened, they would deal with it. Whereas I'd rather pour oil on troubled water any time, particularly right now. So, I decided not to act. And it naturally diffused.

Handling strains in relationships

I think it's fair to say that most relationships, however loving and congruous, have moments of tension. My learning from personal experience and the stories I have heard is that these conflicts cause us suffering on some level – whether that is sadness, distress, anger, frustration, or a whole range of other emotions. Our self-talk is more likely to be critical than kind to ourselves.

Exchanging stories with my interviewees and discussing personal triumphs as well as difficulties in the CCW Community (see page 6) has taught me how to show self-compassion and notice how I'm feeling in the moment. I tell myself that I'm not alone and that it is OK to feel whatever emotion it is. This practice has stopped me ruminating for hours about the things I should have said and done, and helped me to accept my limitations and move on. I cannot change what is past; I can shape the future, however. This reminds me of the first part of the Serenity Prayer by Reinhold Niebuhr, which we visited during one of our recent Community discussions:

> **Father, give us courage to change what must be altered, serenity to accept what cannot be helped, and the insight to know the one from the other.**[13]

The following stories allow us to witness individuals who have responded differently to being hurt or taken for granted, and consider what accounts for the difference. As you read them, think about your close relationships and how you handle tension in them.

We will begin with Beatrice, who was expecting her first child. When Beatrice discovered that she was having a daughter, this caused her to reflect on her relationship with her own mother. Beatrice was able to express compassion and wisdom towards her mother and her siblings, recognising that they had done the best they could, and to combine these Three Companions to reach out to her estranged mother:

> I grew up in difficult circumstances and had to be older much sooner. I've also played a mother figure to my siblings. My husband had a very different, loving, home environment. It's made me see my family in a different light and offer forgiveness and compassion. Understanding that they didn't have the best examples, where they were in life was different and that sometimes a person can only give you so much. You have to understand that that's all they have and know. Being able to forgive, that was compassion.
>
> My husband and I have talked about the difficult relationship I have with my mother. When we found out we were expecting a baby girl, I found her and reached out. I let her know I was expecting and how that made me reflect on our relationship. And I'm so grateful for everything she's done for me; I wouldn't be the person I am without her. She didn't respond. The compassion there was, being the person to reach out. I know that she received that message, and it did something for her healing. I didn't do it because I needed a response or I had an expectation, but because I had the compassion for whatever she may be going through in her life. It didn't allow her to connect with me. That compassionate moment happened very recently and it's in my mind because it's something I've struggled with throughout my life. Being able to change that tide a bit and have compassion for her perspective, or why things are the way they are, is a big example.

I could never imagine not being in my daughter's life or hurting her and her not understanding why. All the things that you struggle with as a child, especially in a mother and daughter relationship. Having my own child was a push for me to reflect on what kind of role model I want to be – both to celebrate the positive things about me that are a direct result of my mother, and the things that I want to change. Then to voice that and do something about it. I guess, not see the whole situation as negative. The good and the bad that happened leads to where I am right now.

The next example describes a similar realisation that parents are fallible human beings who have their own suffering to deal with. Sabina told me about her relationship with her father:

I never had a good relationship with my dad growing up. I only found out why when I was a teenager. We had a hard time connecting. When I finally reached a point where I could understand why, it was so much easier to let go of that anger or frustration I had had for a long time.

'So how did you get that understanding of him?' I asked.
Sabina replied:

I think it's when people grow up. When you're younger, your world is small and in the centre there's you. All the focus that you have shifts onto yourself and what's happening to you. The whole world is against you. It's never about other people. When you grow up, I think your view widens so much that you see behind things and think about what this thing means for the person they're coming from. You realise that some people are in different situations, and they have a whole life story behind them that you probably don't know. When I understood that, I had conversations with my dad without the anger or feelings that could spark a bad conversation. We had nice conversations, putting everything aside, and with love. It was so much easier to connect with him. I feel like people can find connections when they're more understanding and able to listen.

Maja was similarly able to use the Three Companions in how she handled the situation with the person who caused her pain:

I showed extraordinary compassion, and for the first time really understood what it meant six months ago. A friend did something that hurt me, my stepchildren and my friends. I knew it was nothing to do with him; he has mental health challenges. I have known him four to five years and he has shown me kindness. He has many demons and suffers from PTSD. He had tried to lie his way out of what he had done.

I met him for a coffee, with a friend who was there as a witness. I radiated compassion – no anger, judgement or bitterness. I said, 'I don't hate you. It's important for you to tell the truth for your mental health.' After 40 minutes of denial, he admitted it. My friend said later, 'I don't know how you did it.'

It was a life-defining moment for me. I didn't believe I could do it and I am so glad that I did. I am so glad that I found a way through. It was more than unconditional love.

I think Maja showed immense courage and wisdom here as well. She told me it was incredibly hard to sit through his denials. Instinctively, she knew that she needed to give him the space to confess and enable them both to heal.

Sometimes friends lack the awareness to realise that their actions are self-centred and inconsiderate, as the following stories show. In this first one, we are nearly three years on from when Denise's brother-in-law died; she explains how somebody really offended her:

My sister didn't celebrate Christmas in 2017 or 2018, but Christmas just gone, she decided that she wanted to do something. She wanted to go to the Lake District for one of these Christmas breaks where everything's done. She persuaded me to go.

I mentioned it to a friend of mine. She went, 'That's only about an hour-and-a-half drive from me. That's a good option for me because my boyfriend will be away.' But I hadn't invited her.

So I had to say to my sister there'd be another person at our table on Christmas Day. I thought, 'Her family don't live in this country. She seems to have fallen out with her best friend. She'll be on her own for Christmas Day.' So, compassion was not telling her to get lost; you've not been invited.

On Christmas Eve, my friend phoned me and said, 'My boyfriend's coming back so he might be joining us.'

I said, 'Joining us? There's no us. If he's coming, can you make your own arrangements because I don't want to force my sister to spend Christmas dinner with two strangers? This is time that she's put aside for us.'

I lacked courage because I didn't tell her straight. What I should have said was, 'She didn't invite you. We're putting up with you because it's Christmas. If your boyfriend's coming, you'll have something to do so please bug off and let us have our own space.'

By the time we got there, she had phoned me again and said, 'It's all decided. I'm going to come and have lunch with you. He'll do something with his family for lunch. Then we'll be four for dinner.'

And I said, 'Hold on, we won't be four for dinner.' I said, 'No. If he's coming, you will have company for dinner. So, we'll go back to being our two. We'll meet you for a drink in the bar before Christmas dinner and then if you two do your own thing, I'd appreciate it.'

She joined us for lunch, as agreed. Later, when we went down to the bar for dinner, they weren't there. Then the boyfriend turned up, introduced himself and said, 'She's at the table.' So, we walked through, and she had changed our table to a four. I was really annoyed. I thought: 'You showed no respect for my boundaries.' I feel annoyed with myself that I haven't been able to articulate that to her because I feel mean. But I think that she had a bloody cheek showing up.

Isla has also been pushed to the limits by a friend who has trampled over her boundaries for years. The ski holiday that we hear about was the last straw for Isla:

I'm not showing much compassion, courage or wisdom with my friend now. I haven't seen her for a year. She keeps asking to come over and stay and I keep saying I've got too much on. That is absolutely showing no courage. I've given so much for so long to her and it's just taken for granted.

The ski holiday we had last year, we said she could come with one nephew. She came with two and we didn't have enough accommodation. She expected us to give up our rooms. She's hard to fight because she's a big personality and she always gets what she wants. It was really hard work for me, and there doesn't seem to be any understanding of the impact she's having. And now, I have been pushed too far.

If I was compassionate, I would sit down and explain nicely how I felt. I've been a huge part of that problem. I've let her do stuff without saying, 'That doesn't work for me.' I tend to give a lot and I don't mind, but when people start to expect a lot, I start to resent it. So, I'm not being compassionate to her. I'm not able to see things from her perspective. And part of me thinks, 'I can't be bothered. I don't want to.' Those thoughts aren't compassionate. They aren't showing courage and they're certainly not showing any wisdom.

I recognise the situations that both these ladies are in: being annoyed with their friends and not feeling able to speak up and tell them. Showing courage, compassion and wisdom is definitely not the easy option. However, having a rift in a friendship also consumes a lot of energy and we often beat ourselves up for not having the honest conversation.

In this next story, Amanda and her husband took the decision to move away rather than confront a difficult neighbour:

We moved to High Wycombe from a house I really loved that we'd done up. We had a very odd neighbour. She started playing up. We had a dog, and he used to bark at the postman. She got it into her head that he was barking for 24 hours so she reported us to the council, who then used to sit outside our house. It all got very stressful. At the same time, I was getting ill. She carried out more than one vendetta. In the end we moved.

There was always a part of me that felt like a coward because I'd moved away from it. We moved because we thought she was poisoning the dog. I think now, in hindsight, it was OK. I had a good business going there so that might have also been part of her bugbear. The council said, 'You're not going to win this one because the law is set on the side of the complainant. There isn't a law for you, even if you're innocent.' So, we did move and I'm glad we have. But when I look back, I think we should have tackled it another way.

Disputes with neighbours can become emotionally charged and extremely stressful. I have witnessed this on several occasions. It's very hard to see the world from your neighbour's perspective when it feels like they are making your life unpleasant. Home is a place to find peace and be at ease, where we can relax and be ourselves. I think this is why it is so distressing when we get into conflicts with our neighbours. In hindsight, Amanda's accumulated wisdom now tells her that engaging in dialogue with her neighbour might have been a better way to deal with this difficult situation.

In this next example, Eleanor felt hurt when a good friend, who had supported her during her first bout of cancer, was not there for Eleanor when she had a second cancer. This led to a distance between them. She takes up the story:

A friend who is a therapist was very compassionate towards me when I had my first cancer. When I had my second cancer, she wasn't there. I found that really difficult because she's somebody who I have supported a lot and she had supported me earlier. I've listened to all her problems throughout the year. I began to feel rather hurt. I didn't reveal how I felt. There was an estrangement between us, which was driven by that, but I think she never knew why. In the last couple of years, we've come back together again.

If we feel hurt by someone's behaviour, it is very hard to reach out. We wonder why they are behaving that way, and what have we done to deserve such treatment. I know that when I feel hurt, I withdraw into myself. It can take some time before I can see their perspective and the part that I play in the relationship dynamics. Eleanor was able to reach out to her therapist friend for help, which was a natural way of re-kindling the friendship.

When I asked her, 'What brought you back together?' she told me:

I've been through two or three years of problems with my youngest son. He is a clinical psychologist. He went through a near breakdown because of his work. He worked with kids in care and had five suicidal women simultaneously. One of them committed suicide after he had to put her into a psychiatric unit. She committed suicide on his 40th birthday. It turned nasty because the system was falling to bits. He lost his job. So, I went through a hellish time through all of that. I took it upon myself to tell my friend and she was excellent. She understood because she knows the field. She knows how psychologists can be to each other.

'And what made you reach out to her?' I wondered.

Eleanor replied: 'That's a very interesting question. I knew she came from the field and might have something to say about dealing with it.'

Part of our wisdom is knowing how to show someone else compassion in a way that is right for them. Eleanor felt she showed compassion by reaching out to her friend for advice and so allowing her to become close again. It probably took courage to do that, as her friend could have rejected this direct appeal for help.

Milly's story reveals how complex family history and unresolved issues can resurface with devastating consequences:

After my grandfather died, I was very involved in the care of my grandmother, who was then living on her own and suffering from progressive dementia. I live in London, and she lived about 15 minutes away. My father lived in Winchester. He was travelling up every week. I was the person on the spot. She had an incredible network of carers; very expensive at a time when funds were running out. It was a difficult and incredibly time-consuming scenario.

My parents had a very ugly divorce when I was 11. My dad had been having an affair and is still married to the woman he was having the affair with. She is a difficult person. My brother and I made our peace with her. My mum and dad couldn't ever be in the same room, etc. So, it was a difficult family constellation to grow up with. As my grandmother became more senile, she forgot how to be civil to my stepmother. She became increasingly outspoken about her dislike of her, which she had never voiced previously.

My stepmother said, 'What would you say about finding your grandmother a care home to live in that is near to us in Winchester?'

I said, 'I think it would be a good idea to try it for a month.' If it worked, it would be fantastic. And even if it didn't, we would be able to move her back into her house

121

with a saner structure of care that would be affordable for the next five years.

We eventually found this place. I had a bad instinct about it but thought that was likely to be my feeling about any care home. It was only 15 minutes away from my dad's. He went to see her every day and I tried very hard to visit. We decided that we could also pay for some supplementary care, somebody to come and be with her. I rang a lot of agencies in Winchester, and we would always hit this barrier. Eventually they would talk to my stepmother, and she'd cock it up. It was my stepmother's revenge.

After a short holiday I went to see my grandmother. By then she'd been there for three weeks. I was absolutely appalled at what had happened to her. I will never get over the state she was in. You've got to understand that this was a woman who was beloved by everyone. She had devoted her entire life to the care of others. It was this horrifying moment where I thought, 'Look at her. There are no guarantees.' Because she had one enemy and that person was in an utterly crucial pole position. I was shocked.

I went home and rang my dad. I said, 'We talked about this being a one-month trial, I've been to see her, and I am horrified at what's happened. I would like to start planning with you how we sort her home out so that she can come back in a way that's sustainable and sane.' Obviously, he felt terrible. He was out of his depth. He was besotted with his mother and she was in an awful state. He started making excuses for the home. I said, 'She brought you up to expect things to a certain standard. Is the way she's living all right? Is that what we expect? Is that the standard?'

There was this long silence and he said, 'I'll put your stepmother on the phone.' And he handed the phone to my stepmother who just shouted at me. She had never shouted at me before. Just shouted and shouted at me and would not listen.

I remember I put down the phone and said to my husband, 'I can't. It's taken away from me.' My dad left us for her in the first instance. I thought, 'Wow, I've come to that moment again. If I push it, I know which way his decision goes.' There was nothing to stop me sorting out her house, getting the staff, picking her up in my goddamn car and bringing her to London. But it would have been a declaration of war and I have no idea how it would have gone from then on.

I rang my brother, who said, 'I will support you whatever you do, but I will not get involved.' I felt we were both slightly disabled by the fact we'd never resolved it the first time around, that we experienced this sort of ineffectualness as children. And now, we were back at the same point.

It's not a pure regret, I don't think of a moment where I feel, 'Damn, I should have done that thing and I didn't.' But I do feel somehow, if I'd kept nibbling at it, there should have been a way not to allow myself to be disabled by my past. Maybe wisdom was where I failed. Maybe compassion for my stepmother would have helped. Sometimes where someone is driving you mad and you're thinking this person is evil, giving them some love will defuse the situation.

There was a real fear of testing that relationship with my father. Included in that was a fear of breaking the image that I have for myself of our family and who we are – all the generations of the family – because that's tremendously important to me. We're all very close, and yet at the middle of it is this huge chasm, which we have all grown around. And I was scared to destroy that. Didn't want to go there.

I have a sense of the powerlessness that Milly felt. It is tough to go against a parent, especially when there is some fragility in the relationship. On the surface, it might seem idyllic, but we won't have to dig too far to discover the cracks.

Helping others

Unsurprisingly, the Three Companions often show up when we are helping others. There have been many occasions when I have tried to help someone, only for me not to get it right. For example, it has taken me a while to learn how to best support my daughter.

My daughter and I are close. She has called me at times when she is in distress over relationship issues or problems at work. In the past, I would listen and desperately want to help her. I wanted to wave a magic wand to take her problems away, but I couldn't. I would offer my advice and sense that this was not what she needed because she would reject it. I did not use my skills to help her figure out what she could do. I think we both left those calls feeling dissatisfied – me because I couldn't help, she because I couldn't help. I have learnt that by calling on my Three Companions, we have more rewarding conversations. I listen more attentively because I'm not worrying about how to help. And I acknowledge how she's feeling. She feels supported because I am fully there for her, and she feels a sense of release. So, I am helping through my supportive presence.

I think part of the shift in these conversations is that we have both grown as individuals, which has helped us meet each other in this aspect of our relationship. I like to think that we are responding to each other through our use of courage, compassion and wisdom.

In some of the interviews, my interviewees and I reflected on how the Three Companions enable us to focus more on others. If we do that, we tune in to what they require from us rather than what we want to give. The stories that I feature here are a mix of situations in which individuals were able to use the Three Companions and those circumstances where they didn't. It's thought-provoking to explore the differences between those times when my interlocutors were able to help and when they chose not to.

Let's first look at some examples of where people were able to show courage, compassion and wisdom by taking action that provided opportunities for others. Aiden worked for a UN agency and his first posting was in Bosnia and Herzegovina. He takes up the story:

When I arrived in Sarajevo in '97, the first place I stayed in was opposite the orphanage. Three kids from there were annoying me so fucking much. On Saturday they would come at eight in the morning and ring the doorbell asking did I have any money. So, I said, 'The deal is, you have to cut the grass or wash the car or something like that. And you're not getting any money. I'm taking you for a burger and French fries somewhere.' And I said, 'Anybody who calls before midday, no burger for the next three weeks.'

The smartest of them was Srdjan. Srdjan used me as his guardian. He asked me to go to his school because he had got in a fight with some Roma kids, so I went, reluctantly. Srdjan knocked on the door of the teacher's staffroom, and a woman came out and said to him, 'What you want?'

He said, 'I'm here to see Sebija.'

She said, 'She's having her coffee, come back later.' She turned around and walked away. But the door of the staffroom swung open so that they could see me, and Sebija immediately jumped up and said, 'Oh, I didn't realise you were here with a foreigner.' She came to the door, immediately apologised, and said there had been a little trouble with Srdjan. It was totally bizarre.

Anyway, he hated that technical school and I ended up collecting money for him from my friends so he could go to film school in Wales. I got all my friends to give 500 euros a year each to get the £7,000 we needed per year. He's 35 now, so that's a 20-year investment producing a happily married idiot with a British passport, a successful business, and a child and a wife.

These guys are orphans. They've been through a war. Let's be decent. Let's see what we can do.

These next two stories are also about enabling others to get an education by paying for something essential in their lives that made it possible. Grace is now living in the UK and is still connected to her home in Africa. She highlights the precariousness of life and opportunities where she comes from:

One time I was here [in the UK], and my mum called. We're talking, and she said, 'I've just come back from hospital to see Danso.'

I said, 'Why? What happened to him?'

'He had an accident, and we don't know what's going to happen. The doctors can't operate on him because he and his family have got no money.'

This guy had three daughters and he was the only breadwinner. He was in his twenties then, doing his very best. He was educating his daughters. That's not a thing that happens a lot in my world, or which people take for granted, especially when they don't have enough. He didn't have much, so it was easy for him to not educate his kids. And I thought if this man dies, these kids are not going to get an education. I asked, 'Do you know what's going to happen?'

'Oh, well, we don't know,' Mum replied. 'The doctors have said if by tomorrow morning we don't have money, there's no operation on him and that's probably it.'

I don't know whether you call it compassion, but I thought, 'If I had not had an education, I would be married with 17 children.' I'm not saying that's not a good life, but it wouldn't have been my life out of choice. And I thought if these girls' father dies, they have no choice of life. I know for sure that will not be a good life. So, I said, 'Could you find out how much it is and give them the money? Then I'll pay for it.' I wasn't saving his life; I had compassion for these girls.

And when he said, 'How can I pay you back?' I said, 'You don't need to pay me. All you need to do is make sure these three girls go to school for as long as they need to.' I think that is compassion.

In a similar fashion, Martina paid for childcare so that a mother could continue her education:

I decided to use my privilege of having an income to give money to a friend who doesn't, having been here for 10 or 12 years and lost all her family and everything. She has a child who's now seven. She's done three years at university; she's now doing a Masters. Her English isn't great. It's really hard. Before COVID, she was struggling to pay for the childcare. So I'm paying for the childcare, which is easy because I've got the money. But underneath it is my relationship with her, which is where the compassion is.

'Say more about that,' I prompted. 'I'm wondering what is underneath that act?'

Martina explained:

It's a little bit of a maternal thing, interestingly. I've never thought of it like this before. She doesn't have anybody. She's got loads of friends. She's a member of her Church, full of people from her country, people she's known. She's got lots of people in her life. I've never been able to have something of that connection, which is why I want to be there for her. I see her a few times a year. We don't have lots of time together. So, I'm not a grandmother to her child. But she knows I'm there and that's the main thing. She knows she can pick up the phone if she's in trouble and I will do my best to help.

Washid was a university student when we spoke, and a hall senior; that is, he provided pastoral care for the students living in the same hall. He recounts going into the kitchen and finding a distressed student:

She's sitting in the kitchen alone in the dark. I say, 'Hey, are you OK?' She turns around and sees me. She's got super red eyes. She's obviously not fine but I don't want to push, so I start cooking and then she starts to talk.

That leads into her talking about some problems she's having, about pressure. She's from an Asian background as well. Her parents have made her play piano and stuff like that. And she feels guilty for not maintaining that at university. I was trying to give some advice about that. And she starts crying. That was a very uncomfortable situation for me because I've not dealt with anything like that before. She runs out, and then she comes back in.

I asked, 'Do you want to talk about it?' That's the first time I've been able to share some wisdom, because I said, 'Is it really the piano that you're worried about?'

She said, 'No.' It was about stuff that I related to in my first year. She felt like she didn't belong in university; she didn't deserve to be there. So I was able to share what I've been through as well. She's so much more confident now, which is nice.

Four powerful stories of individuals seeing persons in need and doing what they could to support them. What I particularly like is the selflessness of their acts, purely focused on enabling the recipient in some way that honoured their dignity.

We can use our Three Companions to perform small acts, as well as life-changing ones. Josie was quick to help a lady in her sixties who had a minor accident:

> I remember someone fell in my road. That's a very small example of courage, of compassion. They are all interconnected. Her handbag got caught, I think, as she was coming out of her car, and she fell flat on her face. I felt the need to act because I was right there and could help. Also, they are Latin American, I speak Spanish, so I can converse with her in her own language. The wisdom, I guess, is that you can help by being there, or calling somebody or getting medical help. Courage to do what was the right thing morally. She was super grateful. So that's why she came up to me to thank me even though this was months later.

On the other hand, Fernando became desensitised to many of the homeless people in the city where he lives, because it is such a huge problem. Sometimes he ignores them and walks past. However, he has an inner dialogue in which he questions his actions:

> Homelessness is a serious issue in the nation's capital. Sometimes walking down the street, in a couple blocks, you are approached by three or four homeless people who ask you for money. To a certain degree, you become desensitised to the issue. There are times where someone asks you for some money or something to eat and you just walk by and ignore them. Then you think, 'Would it hurt me to stop and give them $1?' But you tell yourself, 'If I did that for every single one on my way to work, I would probably hand out $6 or $7.' Then you say, 'Should I feel bad for even saying or thinking that?' Sometimes I stop. There's one that lives literally on the corner of the building where I work. I talk to Ethan almost daily, and I give him money all the time.'

'So, what got you into talking to Ethan?' I wondered.

Fernando told me:

What got me to talk to Ethan was he was very nice and appreciative. To me, that makes a difference. There are times where I give, and they don't say thank you or show appreciation. That's like a slap in the face. It makes me regret doing it. Ethan was a nice guy. He was very appreciative. I decided to 'invest a little bit more time in him'. Ethan was articulate and sincere. He asked me my name. Rarely would you come across a homeless person where you spark a conversation. That's initially what got me to befriend him.

Fernando went on to explain that there were different reasons why he did not always help them: 'Sometimes I could give them a buck or acknowledge them, rather than completely ignore them. I know that that's been an experience a multitude of times.'

I asked, 'What is it that stops you from acknowledging them and giving them the dollar?'

He explained:

Multiple things. When we lived across the street from Union Station, I would walk across the street. It's a popular place for the homeless. To get to the metro entrance, I came across nine or ten of them. If I had stopped for everyone, I would have to leave an extra ten minutes. I hate to say it like that. Sometimes I help one or two, but I can't help 20 people on my way to the metro.

I have to survive and make sure that I'm taking care of my wife and child. You can't help others at the total cost of yourself. You have to keep your health and well-being to make sure that you can help others.

Some are very, distasteful and rude, and expect you to give them money or help them. If you're asking for help, you must come from a place of gratefulness. Sometimes you don't have the time. Sometimes you don't feel like it. Sometimes you don't have any money on you, and don't feel like explaining that to them.

There are several reasons. It's never been from a spiteful place or that they don't deserve it. It's more of an inconvenience factor or desensitisation of just constant exposure.

Fernando highlights an important point. We can't help others at the expense of ourselves. It's the oxygen mask analogy in the airplane safety speech. I also recognise my behaviour in what he says. I am ashamed to say that I do not acknowledge homeless people very often because I can't or don't want to help. I also feel embarrassed and guilty about my decision, so it's easier to walk by and ignore them. I have recently learnt that often what homeless people want is to be acknowledged. I try to greet them more often but feel uncomfortable about doing that while not donating.

Fernando's story also illustrates three conditions that enable us to show courage, compassion, and wisdom: self-care, self-compassion and values. We need to feel resourced to help others. When we feel depleted, our actions then may seem like a sacrifice rather than a service. His self-talk was an aspect of self-compassion. When we or others do not act in line with our values, it is hard for us to use our Three Companions. I detected that one of Fernando's own values is about people being humble and appreciative rather than feeling entitled.

The next story is about Henry's reactions to different homeless people:

I'm pretty confident I have shown acts of compassion in my life. They tend to be specific and memorable; for example, when I gave 20 quid to a homeless man. I don't think compassion can exist without action. There's a difference between that and feeling kind thoughts. Three weeks ago, I got off the train. It was chucking it down with rain. There was a guy asking for money. I didn't have any coins, but I had a 20-pound note. I often walk past and say, 'I'm sorry, I haven't gotten anything.' I know that's not true. On this occasion, I thought, 'I can't say anything because I know I've got 20 quid.' So, I gave him 20 pounds.

The act of giving him 20 quid wasn't a compassionate thing to do. That was just giving money away. Thinking, 'Blimey, he's got such need; isn't this terrible? Why would he be possibly homeless? God, I can't begin to conceive what his world's like', and linking the two together, that's compassion. It's feeling and acting in a way that demonstrates something that's over and above kindness. I felt, 'I've done the right thing. In two hours' time, I won't remember that I had 20 pounds in my wallet. Whereas he might be warm and in a shelter.' I felt it was the decent thing to do. It was the right thing to do. And I felt I was fortunate enough to be able to do it.'

I interpret the reason Henry felt compelled to show compassion on this occasion was due to integrity; he didn't want to lie to the homeless man about not having any money. And yet, Henry does not feel this way towards every homeless person he meets.

I asked him, 'Can you think of an example where you haven't displayed compassion?'

He replied:

The homeless person I walked past the other night. Why was I compassionate to one and not the other?

I was in a hurry. They're always there. They're often kneeling with their head in their hand, and their sign saying, 'I'm hungry.' It's a desperate thing, but I walked past.

What was going on for me? There's a permanence about their presence. I was used to them being there, therefore it didn't strike me. So, an 'they must be all right' assumption.

It sounds a terrible thing to say, but there it is. My thoughts were more self-centred. I showed more of the selfishness trait. I was thinking about myself and showed less compassion.

Henry experienced similar desensitisation to that which Fernando sometimes felt. There is a fine balance between being self- or others-focused. Compassion can be directed towards ourselves as well as others. I think that using the Three Companions means that we need to tune in to ourselves, notice what is happening and question how we feel about that. Sometimes, like Fernando, we will focus on our needs. At others, we will feel sufficiently resourced to give our attention to people in need. The more that we can accept our limitations, the more we can celebrate the times when we do use the Three Companions, rather than punish ourselves on the occasions that we don't.

Camila wanted to offer her services to a charity at Christmas by volunteering to help. However, they did not need her. When she examined her motives, it was about her feeling wanted:

When my husband and I first split, we were alternating Christmases. One Christmas he had our children, so I was on my own for the day. I decided to generously give of my time to a charity. It turns out it was all for my own benefit. There's a charity called 'Help the Family'. They had a respite place where they brought families together to try and work together.

It took me some courage to go. I arrived at this place. Bear in mind that I'm an experienced professional. I work with these sorts of people and families. But I was put to do the Brussels sprouts in the kitchen and expressly told not to talk to any of the families because that required experience, knowledge, insight, etc. People made polite conversation with me but basically: 'Put out the sprouts.'

I did that for a couple of hours. Then I went for a walk up on the Clwyds and felt a complete fool. I had thought that it was going to look good, rather than stay at home and feel sorry for myself. But I realised that I had intruded on a space that wasn't mine. I had tried to do something to make myself feel better but I felt a lot worse because it felt very half-hearted. With reflection, it was not wise. If you're going to do that you need to show more commitment.

Next, we meet Amelia, who talks about the courage and compassion it takes for her to volunteer over the Christmas period at centres supporting people experiencing homelessness and what she has learnt in doing so:

I've found I've needed a lot of courage and compassion when I have volunteered at the centres. I found that difficult to start with. It's not easy because I don't relate to the people. You're helping people who are living rough on the streets and homeless. Until now, thankfully, I've never been in that situation. I'm lucky. I haven't had an addiction to any substance, been thrown out of my home, or been unable to earn money or hold a job down or whatever it is.

So, I found that a very good thing for me to do. To take time to try and understand people, support them or just relate to them as people. And it's changed me. One thing I've been told is that when someone is sitting on the street, people just walk by them. I make a point, now, of making eye contact or talking to them. I don't give money. I'll help in other ways. I will treat them as a person.

Martina admitted that fear of COVID-19 prevented her from checking if a homeless person needed help. This was an emotion that featured in a lot of the stories. This makes sense because the definition of courage (see page 19) is acting despite fear. When asking people about times when they did or didn't display the Three Companions, it is reasonable to expect fear to show up. Martina explained:

Two days ago, I got out of my car and there was a homeless man asleep up on a grass bank under a tree. I thought, 'I wonder if he's asleep or if he's dead?' I'm a bit ashamed of this because I chose not to check. When I came back to my car, he'd gone. So, I presumed he was asleep. But I'd made the choice not to go check. It was about COVID and the risk. That wasn't compassion.

Another condition for showing courage, compassion and wisdom is defining and maintaining our personal boundaries. When we do that, we can give help more easily without feeling taken advantage of. Roger's story exemplifies this:

There was a chap of similar age, who I met a couple of years ago in the gym. We had a warm but passing relationship. It was quite nice, a bit remote, but fine. I'd call him up from time to time, 'How're you doing?' He was funny, I enjoyed his company, and he was helpful.

In January, he said, 'I've a terrible problem. I've lived in my house for 37 years and I've eventually decided to sell the house.' Then the story started evolving that he was in a bad way.

I said, 'What's happening?'

'I fell down the stairs two days ago, hit my head. I'm in terrible pain.'

So I popped round to see him. His house was in a terrible state, a real mess, and so was he. Then I started hearing his life story. I said, 'Who's looking after you?'

'The family, but not really.'

So, I started going round there and taking ready meals. He insisted on paying me, which felt good because then it was a reciprocal thing and not charity. I went maybe ten times – every few days until he moved. I saw him a couple of times after he moved, and he was completely miserable.

Why was that compassion? In a way, I took him on. The thing that I remember about that time was I decided: 'I'm not going to take you on as an entire project because I would be in deeper than I wanted to be. What I can do is pop around, allow you to make me a cup of tea, we have a chat and I'll bring you a ready meal.' Maybe there was wisdom too, self-preservation wisdom. This is the parameter; this is my limit.

My wife said, 'Why are you going?' and I said, 'Well, I just feel for him.'

We can show compassion for all living creatures, not just human beings. Here are two stories about individuals showing compassion for dogs. The first one is from Anna (who earlier shared her story about going to the USA to study):

I am not a dog or pet person. I'm allergic to fur and dust. But it is my luck that every dog in my family has died with me. The latest was the beagle, my daughter's pet. My daughter got her when she was eight; she is now 24. The beagle was super old. When my daughter went overseas, the maid looked after the dog. When my mum died, I sent the maid home. Then I had to look after the dog until she died two weeks ago.

I noticed that the dog was going slower and then she stopped eating. It was just before the start of our pandemic lockdown. I paid for a vet to come and look at the dog. When he wasn't doing any good, I got another one to come. I got them to take her to the dog hospital. Because the dog had been in my family for a long time, it meant a lot to me that the dog was treated with dignity and respect.

So, when the dog was sick, I asked the vet to put her on a drip. He called me: 'It's not helping. She's not eating. We did a blood test, and her organs are failing. With the MCO, nobody's going to attend to your dog. So, what do you want to do?'[14]

I said, 'Why don't you put the dog out of her misery? She's old. She doesn't recognise me anymore. It's gonna be so hard for her because she's not eating. She'll just wither away, and she might be in pain.'

'This is fine, but it'll cost you.'

I told him, 'Money, I can find again. I cannot bear to see the dog suffer. If it was a person and that person was me, I wouldn't want to suffer like that. It would be much kinder because she's had a good life. Why do you want her to suffer in her last days?'

Anna epitomises compassion to me because she still cared about the dog even though it was not her dog, and she was not a dog-lover. Yet she wanted the beagle to die with dignity and not suffer pain.

Ava feels compassion towards every living creature; that's how she's wired. Her love for her dog shines through in her story:

She's a rescue dog and was in a terrible state when we got her. She was about two; that was 14 and a half years ago. She's my elderly girl, who is right beside me here with her head on my knee, which is where she often is to be found. She'd been kicked, beaten, bred from, and dumped. She was in a mess. She didn't know what a ball was. She didn't know what manners were of any description.

She didn't have any of those boundaries that make one secure. So, she's been constant work. For the first two years, she was real, hard work. My other half says that he's never known me to be so patient and tolerant. It was born of all Three Companions, because I believed that she would come good. I had huge compassion for her because it wasn't her fault, and the courage to take her on.

I am ambivalent about animals; I can take them or leave them. I have never quite conquered a fear of dogs and have been bitten by one while out for a run. However, I see how much people love their pets and become attached. So I can imagine the loving kindness that Anna and Ava showed. I wonder how far we go in relating to all living things with courage, compassion, and wisdom? Trees and plants are also living and are a vital part of our ecosystem. Should we be accessing our Three Companions in how we treat them too?

Protecting and defending others

We protect and defend people whom we believe are less capable of taking care of themselves. I feel this strongly as a mother. When my family went through some rough times, I wanted to take care of my children emotionally. I believed that was my role. When I detect vulnerability in someone, I can slip into rescue mode. I want to make things better for them, so I try to protect them from facing uncomfortable situations. This is not always helpful because I am assuming they don't have the strength or capability to deal with whatever difficulty they are experiencing. When I notice this behaviour in myself, I can let go and give them the room to sort things out in their own way.

Some of the stories I heard about protecting others were not about rescuing them in the way that I have just described. They were tales of protecting people physically by stopping fights. It is 21 years since Aiden met the orphans he told us about earlier. So he is older now than at the time of his first story, and he would question whether he has got wiser. Here, Aiden tells us about two episodes when he intervened in fights:

I was walking the dogs to the Presidency. It's a nice park surrounded by an Austro–Hungarian square four metres high. There's a couple of policemen there and a couple of cameras. I pass this group of teenagers sitting on a bench. Next, one of the kids runs by me, kneels in front of my dogs, and says in English, 'Can I pat the dogs?' This is very unusual behaviour.

Then I started hearing, 'I'll do it for you. Hey, you, pussy! I'll suck your mother's dick!'

I turned around and said, 'What's wrong with you?' The other kids started walking towards me. I turned my two dogs around and said, 'He's not coming back to you. What do you want?' Then one of the guys came up to me and I woke up in hospital. He hit me.

I don't like bullies telling young guys what to do in parks. I'm not having my public space threatened by some hooligans. This is one thing where I hadn't learnt a lot. I remember, [as a young man] in Dublin, coming home once from town. It was late. I saw four guys piling onto this guy. I pulled them off and said, 'OK, he's had enough now.' And I said to him, 'OK?'

He said, 'Yeah, thanks.' I turned around and got bumph straight in the face, but it didn't knock me out, just left me with a great bruise.

So, I don't like people getting in my public space and threatening me. I have this reaction to that, which I should be careful of because, if you're 55 and somebody else is 20 and there are three of them, then it's not courageous. Then it's stupid. It's never about me. I don't like to see other people being threatened.

I think that courage without compassion and wisdom can indeed be foolhardy. I think in this case Aiden showed both courage and compassion; two of the Three Companions.

Another instance where Niamh used her Three Companions was to stop a fight without a thought about the potential danger to herself:

I did once stop a fight. There were some young men who were fighting. In hindsight, they'd probably been taking a lot of alcohol. The fight broke out in the road and various neighbours appeared. Mostly, it was flailing at one another. And then one of them was on the floor, and the others were kicking his head. I didn't hesitate because that was not going to go well for anybody. So I intervened and said, 'Stop!' and fortuitously they did.

I don't know if that was brave because I didn't think about it. It was the right thing to do. It also showed compassion for him, or for all of them. It was one of those situations when you either moved and did something, or not. I did, and it turned out fine. He was OK.

Would I do it again? I don't know because most people said, 'You could have been hurt or they could have had a knife.' I hope I wouldn't think of those things and stop, because I think it was the right thing to do for all three of them.

I think in both stories, Aiden and Niamh instinctively did what they felt was right. I don't know that, in similar circumstances, I would have had the courage and compassion to help. I probably would have been afraid for myself, just like those neighbours in the last example.

In the next story, George was afraid of starting a fight if he challenged racist behaviour:

I was in a pub. It's quite a middle-class, white town. Somebody's using the P-word talking about somebody who had come in. I knew that that was wrong. I don't agree with all that. I try my best not to show any form of bigotry towards anything. And I didn't have the courage to tell this guy to shut up. I went home. I felt guilty for a few days after it. There were about 20 people in the bar, and nobody said anything.

What stopped me was that I thought if I said something, it would end up in a big fight. That's what put me off. I was scared to get in a physical fight. Which is why I felt a bit guilty because I've never been in a physical fight I've lost. I never saw this Asian guy again and didn't have a chance to apologise to him for it.

George's behaviour was out of kilter with his values, and he felt uncomfortable about that. If he had acted in accordance with them, he might have been able to draw on his Three Companions to speak out.

Dealing with crises

Crises call for us to employ our Three Companions. The COVID-19 pandemic is a good example. The world as we knew it was turned upside down. There was a killer virus that we had little protection against, and it was spreading fast. It was scary. In the CCW Community, we processed our emotions and responses to the rapidly changing situation. We learnt about courage, compassion and wisdom both overtly and subconsciously. It took courage to show up to these meetings and reveal our innermost thoughts and feelings. Compassion to be with and support each other. Wisdom to recognise that our participation helped to build our resilience to face this senseless world.

In this chapter, we hear the accounts of how Camila, Lottie and Nathan dealt with their crises. First, here is Camila, who reveals how her Three Companions helped her to take charge of a situation that arose during the London bombing in July 2005:

I'll go for the big one, which was being in London on 7 July when all of London got shut down because of bombs on the Underground. I was teaching at UCL, and people had come from across the country. Some had been staying in London that day, and I had arrived from the North to teach this group of about 20. So, I was in alien territory. I knew the setting a little bit, but I didn't know who was in charge.

As I arrived, it was evident there were only about four of us there and people were late. I didn't know what was going on. And neither did anybody. A few people had come in and one or two of them had heard the Russell Square bomb go off. Mobile signal had gone at this point. A couple of other people were coming in from King's Cross. They had seen people coming out of the Tube with blackened faces. So they were a scared bunch.

I realised very quickly I needed to stay calm and in charge. Not that I knew how to do that, because there wasn't very much information. I do remember two young girls from Scotland saying, 'If something's happened in the Underground, surely because we're over it, we're at risk here?'

And I said, 'Oh, no, it's far too far underneath.' Knowing that that might not be true. Having no clue but thinking I better say that.

We started to try to piece together information. I decided that we couldn't run the course. My job was to keep everybody very calm. We went to look at what food was on the premises. Then I managed to find whoever owned the building. We arranged for people to stay overnight in student accommodation if necessary. I think by about three o'clock, we started to know what was happening. So, the courage I needed was from nine o'clock till three o'clock.

By three o'clock, we knew that it was OK for people in London to start walking. So I buddied people up and asked them to ring each other and then let me know that they had got home. So I got a system in place for that. Then by about four or five o'clock trains started to go. I made sure everybody had gone and then I walked to Euston. It was most bizarre because there were lots of pedestrians, no cars. When we got to Euston, you didn't have to show tickets. You got on a train, and they gave you a sandwich and free drinks. They got us all out of the capital.

I guess it was imposed courage. If I'd done anything differently, it would have been difficult for that particular group. I had to act decisively. The main issue in terms of courage was I didn't know what was going on and nobody knew how we were going to behave. My twin sister from Canada had been trying to ring people in London to see where I was. Obviously, the whole world had been worrying about me. It was only at that point I realised that it had been a demanding day. But as I tell the story, I don't feel hugely courageous about it. I think I was just in a place, and I dealt with it as well as I could.

Camila's attitude is reminiscent of Sofia's earlier, in that they both felt they were just doing their job.

Nathan worked as a teaching assistant in a small school for children with behavioural issues. The children came from difficult backgrounds and could be quite unruly. The staff found it challenging to maintain control. Nathan told me about how he dealt with a life-threatening situation with one of these students:

I was working as a teaching assistant in music. I also would sit in art lessons to help maintain control of the room because they can be quite unruly. And I did one-on-one lessons.

One of the kids that I did this with had a lot of family issues, a very troubled background, been in care and he had psychological issues. He was supposed to be going to the library to prepare for his GCSEs. It was a one-on-one, just after lunch. He had a lot of energy and wanted to be with his friends in other classes. He's a big kid; 16 at the time. I'm trying to get him to go, but he doesn't want to because it's maths and it's boring.

He starts running around the corridors and barging into classrooms. We're taught how to deal with the kids without being physical. You can't restrain them unless they're getting violent, which he wasn't. He was just disruptive. He's bursting into classrooms, not staying long, running out and running around. I'm trying to get him to come with me to the library. After about five, ten minutes, I get the teachers to lock their doors so he can't disrupt them. Now he's looking for something else because he doesn't know how to express himself. That really is the problem. He can't explain why he doesn't want to do the maths or how that makes him feel. So, this is how he acts out.

Someone hadn't locked one of the kitchen doors. He burst into a kitchen, picked up a knife, and started waving it at my throat. The situation was getting quite heated. I talked to him. Calmed him down. Got the knife off him. We went to the library, and we did the maths.

The point was that it was scary. He had a knife at my throat, and he wasn't in control. But I didn't run away. So I guess it was courage. The wisdom was knowing not to try and use force because that wouldn't have helped. It would have made him feel more like he was under attack and threatened. That would have made him react more aggressively and it would have escalated it.

Nathan described the emotions he felt, including fear and anger. He felt threatened, so his amygdala took over and he saw the pupil purely as a danger for a while.[15] He was able to overcome this and use his Three Companions, which led to a good outcome:

In these moments, because of fear, our ego takes over and we see it in terms of what they're doing to us. We think about our experience; it's stressful for us. So, before the whole knife thing, I was thinking it's stressful and it's making life harder. Then you're getting annoyed, angry and pissed off. Then when you're afraid, your ego takes over, and we start to dehumanise people. It comes from our biological instincts.

The compassion was to be aware: 'I might be frustrated. I might be afraid. But what I'm feeling is nothing compared to what he's feeling.' The compassion is recognising that and acting on it. If the frustration makes it feel important, because our emotions are so powerful, it's hard to have the awareness to detach and say, 'Yes, it's frustrating, but it probably feels a lot worse for him.'

I wondered, 'When you were in the situation, did you feel the compassion? Or is it something you've looked at in hindsight?'
Nathan explained:

I felt compassion, but that was not the only thing I felt. It was fluctuating constantly. I was feeling a mix of a lot of positive and negative things. Some moments I had awareness and at other moments I got caught up in my own feelings.

I can't remember the pattern, but in the key moments I was able to act with compassion. I'm not sure if I was feeling it consciously. There was fear; that's the obvious one with a knife. There was frustration. My ego was also feeling under threat because I'm supposed to be a man. I can't even deal with this 16-year-old. Then I guess there's a feeling of insecurity – maybe other people would have handled it better or quicker by now.

There was also empathy. At one point, when he was busting into classes, it was irritating but also amusing me because I could see myself in him. I remember being a teenager and wanting to be anywhere but class. So you start acting out; it's not malicious. You're not thinking about the effect you have on other people. So, there was a part that amused me.

There were times when I raised my voice. Culturally, that's what you do to control unruly kids; you're stern. I wasn't thinking about the specifics of the situation, and how he's gonna respond.

And I spoke to him gently and calmly, like a peer, not condescendingly. Because, in those moments, I saw something in his eyes that I empathised with – probably fear, or hurt.

That made me, while still recognising him as a threat, see him as he really was, which was a scared kid who's hurt.

I am impressed at the courage and honesty that Nathan displayed in his retelling of the incident. He was in his early twenties at the time. While Nathan was afraid, he succeeded in connecting with the pupil in a way that took the heat out of the situation, and they were able to go to the library. Such courage, compassion and wisdom at a young age! I don't think I would have been able to go to the library in those circumstances; I would have been too shaken.

Lottie was very unhappy; she had put 200 per cent into her job with little recognition and had clashed with her manager. So she resigned. Then, her manager quit suddenly and failed to turn up for his shift. Lottie felt such loyalty to the team that she put aside her misery and stepped up to lead them. Weekends were always extremely busy and she rallied her staff to pull together as a team. She explains:

When the store manager quit unexpectedly, I felt I needed to step up for the team. So, I said, 'Guys, I know there's lots been happening, people have been talking a lot, but let's all stick together. Let's ignore the rumours and get through this weekend.' I was feeling horrible at the time. I didn't want to be working in the shop as I'd quit as well. But I didn't show that to anybody because it was tough enough.

He was supposed to be working a shift that night. I had been on a training course during the day. He had been on holiday for the three weeks prior to this. I had done 90 hours extra. I was exhausted. I remember saying, 'I'm gonna have to go in and cover his shift.'

People said, 'Why do you have to? Why do you need to step up?'

I really didn't want to, but I couldn't leave it. I cared too much about the shop and about the people. I felt I couldn't just leave. It was a natural thing for me to do.

In all three examples, Camila, Nathan and Lottie were concerned for the people in their care. This focus on others was vital in coming through the crisis in the best way possible. They displayed courage, compassion and wisdom in spades.

Resolving dilemmas with ethics and integrity

There are many times when we are faced with dilemmas, which, by their very nature, are not easy to resolve. I tend to be decisive; however, there are occasions where I want to do the 'right thing' but struggle to do so because this would impact me adversely.

I have mentioned earlier how, in the last two years of his life, my late husband created a toxic environment in our home. His drinking was out of control, and he was angry. I felt threatened and was on high alert all the time. I wanted to show him compassion and help him, and gave him a lot of support and care, particularly when he was sick. I tried to persuade him to get medical treatment, but he refused. Eventually, due to his behaviour, I could not see past how he was making me feel. I could not see that he was in pain, and drinking was his way of numbing that. My dilemma was to either continue living with the man I loved who was making my life hell, or go our separate ways, knowing he couldn't take care of himself properly. I chose the latter. I hoped this would be a wake-up call he needed.

I agonised over this dilemma and took nine months from making the initial decision to asking him to leave. Having courage, compassion and wisdom is an anchor that can help us find the best path for us in the moment. On reflection, I think I did call upon my Three Companions, because I knew that continuing to live in that stressful state would cause me long-term harm. Also, I felt that his having to support himself was the best chance I could give him, everything else having failed, to turn his life around. Sadly, he did not take this opportunity.

The following stories from my interviewees illustrate different ways in which individuals coped with their dilemmas. We'll begin with Belinda, who works with people with addictions and the family members of such individuals. She told me about a distressing case that she had to deal with, where a young man had sexually assaulted his niece. He had no comprehension that this was wrong. Belinda felt conflicted because she was helping someone who had done a terrible thing, rather than condemning him. She resolved this through discussions with her peers so that she was able to use her Three Companions in her interactions with him. She explained:

> In the beginning, he didn't think that there was anything wrong with it. He thought that she was willing, which I couldn't imagine – for she was under 12. I gave him some information about child development. He was never told how you express your feelings. So he was incapable of connecting with people and knowing what was wrong or right. He wasn't taught as a child and he had a very cold home-family situation.
>
> I could feel compassion for him that he was missing life skills and positive experiences. It was very difficult. Although I knew what he was doing, I still had compassion for the drinker [the offender] because there is always something behind that. It's the addiction that does it, so that's what you always try to separate. Then the Three [Companions] come together. Courage to show compassion to him. You show your own experience and what the clinic taught me.

I asked, 'How easy was it for you to be in that situation as a professional and show your compassion?'

Belinda continued:

'I've got supervision with other practitioners at the GP's office. I shared that I was surprised that I could feel compassion for something he did that was so wrong. You feel a conflict with what is right or wrong. I shared that in supervision: 'Shouldn't I be more harsh on him? I should judge more, but that didn't happen.'

It was good to share and learn that not everybody could have a conversation with such a person. So, I felt good about it. There's the child, but I'm not here for the child. I want to protect other children. I have to try to influence him in a way that affects him.

I was proud afterwards that I could share information to prevent him doing this. There was the alcohol abuse that made him more without boundaries. I said, 'Partly, because you did this after a bottle of wine, it's not you but the wine to blame.' It's still his behaviour but maybe the next time he would be aware that after a bottle of wine this could happen.

I was nervous when I saw him on my agenda. I talked with the doctor: 'What is my role? What is the target? Whatever do you want? What is the aim?'

And he said, 'He was a bit agitated because he was not taking responsibility for his behaviour. So maybe he should have somebody to talk with him a bit longer.'

He did feel ashamed afterwards, or maybe during the process too.

Compassion is always unjudgemental: 'What is your story?' I'm there to give him this opportunity and do my best. In the beginning he didn't feel comfortable because he knew that people have judgements about things.

I think this story beautifully illustrates the fact that the Three Companions can be employed in our dealings with people for whom we would normally experience feelings such as antagonism, condemnation and disgust. These feelings do not enable the individual to learn how to behave differently. I truly admire Belinda's ability to show him compassion and, through her courage and wisdom, to help him.

In contrast, Rose realised she was unable to display her Three Companions to a male coaching client because he objectified women. She found this distasteful. You may remember from Leya's story that if somebody's behaviour clashes with our values, it is difficult to manifest courage, compassion, and wisdom. Rose told me:

> It's a long time ago, but it has stuck with me. When I was starting to work in the corporate world, this guy came to me because his boss was concerned about him. He was having an affair with somebody in the business. That affair was impacting his work. His boss said, 'I think you need to help this guy.' I had only three sessions with him. Then I called an end to it.
>
> He talked about his relationships with his wife and this other woman. He wasn't going to give up his wife because he liked the lifestyle that they had.
>
> The third time we met, I said, 'What is it about this woman that you are so enthralled with that you're not working effectively? Presumably your wife knows there's something going on?'
>
> He said, 'We don't have very good sex.' He took out a photograph of a woman on Page 3,[16] and said, 'My lover looks like her.' There was something in the way he looked at me, with anger and resentment and a challenge, which meant it was impossible for me to work constructively with him.
>
> I said, 'Our work is over. There's nothing that I can do to help because you're so fixated on her, and what she looks like.' He was making complaints about his wife being overweight. I closed the book and said, 'That's it, we're done.' And told him to leave. Not a very compassionate thing to do.

'So, what was going on for you?' I asked.

Rose explained:

'The fact that he'd turned her into an object. I felt that it was so disrespectful of both these women and there was something about his integrity. It was because he brought it down to a body that I thought, 'There's no way I'm going to help him to look at anything differently or change.' I didn't want to work with him anymore. I definitely did not feel compassion for him.

I suspect it triggered something in me. I don't want to be looked at as a sex object. Maybe, I compared myself to this Page 3 woman and thought, 'I'm nothing like that. How is he ever going to listen?'

While Rose may not have felt compassion for her coaching client, you could say that she felt compassion for the two women that he was involved with. And it certainly took courage to confront him and to walk away from that engagement. I think wisdom lay in knowing that she would not be able to help him to change.

Jill told me how she did not have the courage to speak out about unethical behaviour by her boss due to fear of the consequences:

I could see that the Chief Executive was painting a picture of business performance that was overly positive to the owners. I didn't raise it with the owners as clearly as I should. I hinted at it rather than facing directly into it. I was the HR Director, so I reported into the Chief Executive but I had a very strong relationship with the owners. They trusted my integrity. I worked hard for that. They also trusted that the Chief Executive would deliver.

He had delivered some very good results. My view was that was largely in spite of, rather than because of him. He had a one-dimensional way of operating, and the world was becoming more complex. The challenges were becoming

157

more complex, and he wasn't being honest about that. It was a tough one for me. I wasn't as direct with my feedback as I could have been. With hindsight I can see and admit that the root of what stopped me was fear. I needed to protect my job. I wasn't ready for the extreme consequences of what might have happened.

I also didn't want to be seen as the person who undermined their boss. The situation was delicate, so I was trying to do a bit of a halfway house, but it didn't work. When the CEO left the company, someone else came in and all that stuff was uncovered. And I'm really frustrated with myself because I didn't speak truth to power then and I could have done. Whether it would have been heard, whether the timing was right, I don't know.

A tough situation to be in. I'm sure that you can relate to being in a position where you knew what the right thing was to do and decided not to do it because it didn't feel safe. Some self-compassion is needed in these circumstances. We can't get it right all the time. All we can do is learn from each situation so that we can step up the next time we are confronted with a similar situation.

Challenging power

A common situation that many of us face involves challenging those people whom we feel have power over us. This can include our parents, teachers, peers, clients and bosses; any person with whom we feel a power imbalance in their favour, can feel difficult to challenge. I illustrated this earlier in my example of showing courage when expressing my discomfort to my own boss (see page 19). I believe that if we can access our inner wisdom in addition to courage, this will tell us what the right thing is to do. Compassion then enables us to do so in a way that doesn't threaten, ridicule or belittle the person in power.

The next two stories are about doing the right thing even if this could have negative consequences for the narrator. The first example is from Aiden:

> You demonstrate courage when you're aware of the risk, and you make a decision on what you think is the right thing to do.
>
> Sarajevo has been the most polluted city in the world – more than Mumbai or Beijing – 10 out of the last 30 days. We have this German project partner, and they know that 50 per cent of the pollution is coming from cars. We're doing a transport project with them. I've said, 'You can't take stakeholders' evaluation where they say they'd like a zero-emissions public transport system and change that to low.'
>
> The head of the German organisation and the project manager don't care. So, we talked to the consultants: 'This is

not what this project is about. It's meant to be about people reducing emissions.'

And they said, 'Oh, come on, you guys.'

So I said, 'I'm going to ask them [German organisation] for some mediation. It's better than arguing with them.'

I went to meet them, and the deputy said, 'What's your problem here?' I explained. She said, 'I just want to make it clear, there's going to be no mediation because we can't afford it.'

I said, 'We'll pay for it.'

She said, 'We have no time for it.'

I said, 'I can't make you have time. But if you want to do it, we're prepared.'

She said, 'If we hear any more about this, you won't get an extension to this project.' For me, it would have been perfectly normal to say 'you can't do this' in reply, but I chose not to.

Our German consultant had a meeting in which the head guy said, 'We're only picking data for the conclusions that we want.' So she wrote an email to the boss.

They wrote back: 'We don't have any problems. If you want to talk to our organisation, please do.'

I waited a long time to see if anyone would say anything. Then I wrote just to the two of them. I've been putting off something which I know I can do. I can have questions asked in the German parliament about the project. I've been putting it off to give them every chance possible.

I said [to my own office], 'Our significant value add is that we will say the things that need to be said. We're not an NGO. We're a think tank because we're trying to create fact-based dialogue. That's why we go through all this. But we're dealing with two people who don't care.'

So, the courage is that you know at the beginning that they're going to cut you off. It's an important part of funding for us. They've given you the warning. Which means I have to evaluate: 'Do I have other projects I can rely on? Is this extremely important to my office to care about this? Do they also feel the same way?'

So, I talked to the staff, because I knew for sure that we would not have funding this year.

Aiden chose to stand by his principles, knowing that it put not only himself but his whole organisation at risk. He told me that the wisdom was not rushing to act as he normally would do but allowing time and space for solutions to emerge.

George encountered many dangerous situations as a tax inspector, including dealing with criminals and having weapons pulled on him. Here he describes finding a potentially huge fine that would significantly affect the company's profit. He had the wisdom to know how to treat this situation to achieve the outcome they needed, but it was not guaranteed. His boss was unconcerned. George had to stand up to his boss to ensure that they were proactive in sorting it out, rather than hoping everything would be fine:

One example of courage was when I was in a role in tax. I came across what was potentially a $1 billion fine. Nobody wants a billion-dollar fine. I knew if it was handled correctly, that you could get it to nothing. I had to go to my boss about that. He said, 'That's a stupid fine, that'll never happen.'

I said, 'It's easy for you to feel that, but if it does happen, it's my butt that's on the line.'

We had a long discussion about it and sorted out where it was coming from. We spoke to some lawyers in America and then to the tax authorities and got out of it all.

It takes a lot of courage to step up for something like that when other people say, 'That's never gonna happen. Shut up.'

I asked him, 'And what enabled you to step up in those situations?' George replied, 'They were straightforward to me because that's right versus wrong. I'm a fair and equitable person. I knew that these were the right things to do. That's what carried me through there.'

Leya now provides us with an example of using the Three Companions at work. Her leadership values clashed with those of her boss. Leya had challenged his behaviour while offering feedback that had yielded only short-term results, so she concluded that she should leave. The way she informed him of her decision was with respect and dignity:

I've been a senior executive of my organisation for a year. It has been a tumultuous year. The CEO wanted to do the right things, but he had some horrific leadership behaviours. Halfway through the year I told him these behaviours have to stop: 'You can't treat your team like that. I won't allow it.' He backed off but then he got anxious and cycled again.

At the end of the year, I resigned. I sent him a letter that I thought about very deeply beforehand. Essentially, I said, 'I love the job. I adore the team. I love the clients. I love working here. But you deserve a senior executive who will do what you want them to do, and I'm not that person. I will never act in a leadership capacity the way that you seem to think is necessary. You and I have diametrically opposed leadership philosophies. I know I will not change. I understand that many of your behaviours are anxiety- and stress-driven. I cannot imagine how painful it is to be inside your head and to feel that all the time. But I cannot stand by and allow you to do that to the team. And I will not allow you to do it to me anymore. You're an adult; you have the responsibility to have some adult behaviours. I will not participate in abusing other people.'

He responded, 'I think I understand the message. What you've said is you love everybody; you don't love working with me.'

I said, 'Yeah, you've got the message.'

He said, 'Will you talk to me about it?'

I said, 'No, I will write to you about what I think needs to be done. It's my gift to you.' And I did this.

He said, 'I understand. I will do these things. We will figure this out because I realise you could have just resigned. You could have screamed at me. You could have used it as a manipulation technique. And you didn't do any of those things.'

I had the courage to say, 'These behaviours have to stop.' I showed compassion. And I had the wisdom to lay it out for him and say, 'This is what needs to be done.' Because I was able to do that in a way that showed compassion and courage simultaneously, and I took myself out of the equation, I was also able to give him the wisdom of: 'As a leader, these are the things I see.'

As a result, he rehired me under the agreement of: 'I [Leya] need to be in a position where when I tell you to stop, you actually stop. If that means I hang up on you because you are out of control, that's what I'm gonna do. I need boundaries that respect me and help you control yourself because I am not going to absorb this any longer.'

It has been good for everybody. And for me, that was about wisdom, compassion and courage – because it takes courage to say no. It takes courage to tell somebody your behaviour is so bad I won't participate in it. And it takes courage to walk away. I had nothing that I was walking into. I knew that I had to do this to maintain my integrity. It was about recognising and acknowledging his suffering, but that even then, I couldn't make it all right for him.'

I agree that it takes a lot of courage to take such a principled stand against your boss. What Leya's story shows is that if we allow ourselves the opportunity to pause and deeply reflect, we can tap into our inner wisdom to take the best path for us at that time.

Lukas was thrown off the leadership team of a country operation of a global organisation, without any explanation, while he was away on a business trip with other colleagues. Lukas felt a sense of injustice and wanted an explanation. Unfortunately, his initial action was not wise, as he realised too late:

> I found out that there was a meeting of the leadership team at my manager's house. The only reason I knew was because I got an agenda off the printer. I didn't know what to do. I put in a call to the Head of Region. This was my boss' boss. Then I thought, 'No, I must talk to my manager first.' So, I called off the meeting. The Head of Region obviously spoke to my boss, who came flying into my office, slammed the door and shouted at me for about ten minutes.
>
> I had the courage of my convictions because there was something not right about the way I'd been dealt with. I didn't have a relationship with my manager that I could go behind closed doors and have a gentle chat. I tried to have compassion for him. I look back and think, 'What if I had spoken to the Head of Region? What would my dialogue have been? What would the outcome have been?' I pulled out of the meeting because I hadn't given my boss a chance to explain. The wisdom was lacking because I should have realised how it looked in a very politicised organisation. But I had a relationship with the Head of Region. I knew him very well personally.
>
> After that shouting episode, I didn't go back to him. Normally, with anybody else, I would have gone back to them and said, 'Let's sit down. Let's clear the air.' I didn't do any of that with him. I saw it as completely fruitless. It would have been an exercise in futility. Very rarely do I get to that point.

I recognise that feeling. Like Lukas, I prefer to have a candid conversation in which both parties reach a deeper understanding of each other. That can only happen if the relationship is founded on trust. I think this was lacking in Lukas's case.

Hugo feared standing up to authority figures; however, he was highly principled. This gave him the courage to confront his boss when he suspected that he wanted to do something unethical:

> My supervisor wanted me to co-sign so he could open a bank account in the association's name. We were both legal signatories. Although he didn't state it, I suspected he wanted to be the sole signatory on the account. This was contrary to our normal practice and policies.
>
> He told me to make an appointment for us at the bank. I knew his mentality and didn't want to talk to him about my concerns beforehand. Otherwise, he would raise a lot of criticism against me: 'How could you think like that? Why do you mistrust my intentions?' So, I was quiet and waited until the moment happened at the bank.
>
> At the bank, we filled out the form. Then he said, 'You can sign here at the bottom.'
>
> I said, 'There's only one signatory listed to operate this account. Are you not going to add my signature? I'm not aware that you have anyone else in mind to be the second signatory. I'm here and we need two signatures on the account.' My voice was trembling because facing up to him as my authority, he was like a surrogate of my dad when I was little. This was a very challenging moment for me. That's why I couldn't bear to raise my voice against him until that moment.
>
> Then he said, 'Are you going to sign?' and I said in a feeble voice, 'No.' He waited for a couple of minutes and then asked me again. Again, I answered, 'No.' Then he walked out of the bank all frustrated. He went one way; I went the other.
>
> I loved the work I did very much, but there are times when you must pay costs to do something right. The financial

policy was dual signatures on bank accounts. I knew it, and he knew it. One of my roles was to have that oversight. We didn't talk about the matter again. But within a couple of months, he transferred me to work elsewhere. That was his retribution. I felt vindicated.

Louise associated courage with confrontation and that was not her style. However, on this occasion, she held out against her boss, who was managing her in a very oppressive manner:

I was managing the child asylum service for a local authority in the South of England. We were looking after them in foster homes and hostels and so forth. My manager wanted to save money and instructed me to use a different section of the Children Act to provide services.

We used Section 17 instead of Section 20. Section 20 is for all children being looked after by the local authority. She wanted to stop that because it was costing too much. She was beautifully mistimed because the Department of Health had said that we were all to use Section 20. I said, 'You are asking me to do something that would be unlawful. There would be huge repercussions.'

My manager was a law unto herself. She said, 'I don't care. I'm telling you to do it.' For her, it was a matter of obedience.

I didn't talk to the director who was her boss. I knew it would drive her mad because she was jealous of the fact that the director and I had a good professional relationship. He thought a lot of me, and she hated that. So, I thought, 'If I go straight to the director, this will add flames to her fire.'

I did spend a lot of time thinking, 'What am I going to do here? How am I going to basically get her to change her mind?'

That resolved itself in an opportune way. A director at County Hall saw me in the corridor one day and said, 'You look awful – what's the matter?' I hadn't slept for about a week.

Out it all came, and I said, 'I'm wondering what on earth I'm going to do because I think I'm going to have to resign. I can't do it.'

And she said, 'Leave it with me.' Well, I know she went straight to the director. They had a word with my boss who then backed down.

The law was useful, let's face it. She was telling me to do something that was going to have a negative impact on a lot of young people who were struggling. So, there were wider reasons for thinking, 'No, I don't want to do that.' There was a point where I just thought, 'If I have to walk away from this job, I just have to take my chances.' It was knowing that it was the wrong thing to do on different levels in different ways and I'll walk rather than do it.

Louise took an ethical stance here. She had compassion for those children seeking asylum. The law was expedient as it helped her to have the courage to stand up to the bullying from her boss. You may remember from the definitions that wisdom emerges from slowing down. Louise refused to act on her manager's instruction, and so gave herself time for a solution to emerge.

Jill felt in a susceptible position because she was relatively new to the Board position that she held. The fear this time did not prevent her from raising her concerns regarding a proposal to a sub-committee of the Board. However, her vulnerability meant that she adopted an unnatural, rational influencing style in which she lost her human side. This harmed her relationships with the Chairs of the Board and the sub-committee for a while. She explains:

I've been working as a non-exec director and I'm a member of one of the Board committees. I bring a different perspective to some of the work that that committee is doing. One of the proposals that came to that committee I didn't agree with. I had spoken to both the Chair of the company and the Chair of the committee beforehand. Both had been robust in dismissing what I thought. I reflected on that and checked out my facts. I thought, 'I've got a couple of options – either let it go the way it's always gone, or take an unpopular stance and raise my concerns.'

I chose to do the latter. It was a tough call because the two Chairs had been in the organisation for a lot longer than I had. What was being done wasn't best practice. I also had the view that it wasn't in the best interest of the broader organisation. It was high stakes to raise it personally because I was also in talks about taking over as the Chair of this committee, and I really wanted to do it. I knew that I would raise doubts in his mind because we weren't aligned in our thinking. But I felt the broader point was more important than my personal position.

I did raise it. It was a tough, emotionally heated conversation. It's taken us a few months to recover, and we're fine now. When I look back, I am proud that I didn't take the easy route. Even afterwards, I held my ground.

What I learnt was, because the stakes were so high, I overly resourced myself with facts and data to support my position, which is not normally how I influence. If I had had more confidence to stand my ground in a way that was truer to me, that would have been a more effective conversation. I lost some of the compassion, which would have come more naturally to me. I knew that it was going to meet a huge amount of resistance and I was dealing with people who are very data driven and fact based. Therefore, I thought, 'Let's lean more heavily into that.'

What would have been more helpful would have been to have relied more on my instincts and leaned more heavily into how I was potentially making them feel. I over-adapted my style to the extent that I lost bits of what would have been helpful. I shifted the balance too far through a fear that if I didn't have my position completely substantiated, then I wouldn't get taken seriously. I should have had more confidence to just be myself.

Denise stepped in to challenge her boss on a conference call that she felt was bullying one of her peers. Her reason is that we don't go to work to be treated that way and that if the boss has a problem with someone's choices, they should tackle that in a private forum rather than in a public meeting. Another example of showing courage, compassion and wisdom at work. She says:

Wisdom is about positive outcomes. I was on a conference call with some colleagues – the guy who heads up our team globally, a counterpart, and our Head of Europe. I could see this global head picking on my counterpart and bullying her. So, I said to him, 'Do you think that this conversation should be had in this meeting?'

When we got off the Zoom call I said to the Head of Europe, 'If he has an issue with how she decides her priorities, that's a one-to-one conversation. I think less of him for having said that in front of us.' The Head of Europe said he agreed. So, I went back to this guy and said, 'Next time we have a meeting, we should agree on what our objectives are in advance. I don't see that it's useful for our stakeholder to hear us challenged about our objectives in meetings.'

If he's got an issue, he solves that before he goes into the room with anybody else. I don't enjoy seeing somebody bullied in meetings and I won't have it. We don't go to work for that. I had nothing to gain by standing up for her. My colleague thanked me. She felt bullied by him and having someone else say it was more powerful because she could never say anything.

I could see the other guy starting to join in. I thought, 'Why is it when anybody's vulnerable, this type of behaviour comes? Let's kill it.' I didn't want any part of it. We're professionals and we're human beings. We don't treat human beings like that.

Confronting powerful people when you are new to an organisation can be scary because you don't know what the repercussions might be. Evie realised that she had an important opportunity to define her relationship with a daunting female executive. This lady was unaccustomed to subordinates questioning her decisions. Evie's action is a form of compassion that is born out of a sense of injustice, which is called fierce compassion. Fierce compassion is what drives individuals to fight for disadvantaged groups and for issues such as same-sex marriage, women's equalities, Black Lives Matter and refugee rights. Evie explained:

I was a support to the senior executive who recruited me. She's intimidating. She is also an anxious person, constantly clicking her fingers: 'I need your best work and I need it now.'

I did a small piece for her. It was rapid and was going to very senior people. She was frustrated with what came back. It wasn't what she wanted. I thought, 'I've got a couple of options here; I can either go, "I'm sorry, I'll try harder. Sorry, my homework wasn't very good." Or I can say to her, "That's a shame. Some good effort was put into this. Maybe I'm not the right person to do this piece of work for you. If you think there's somebody who can pick this up and push it on further and better, let's do that. Because, quite honestly, I feel like I've done everything I can to get it to the place that I have in the time available."'

I chose the latter option. It was a real gamble because I thought, she's going to be really annoyed and try to look for weakness – 'You're just trying to avoid doing that.' But it achieved what I wanted. She said, 'I'm sorry, you're absolutely right. You barely had any time to do this. It's the context you don't know. You've really pulled together the best you can. I don't think there is anyone else who's better to do it. Let me just breathe and let's see what else we can do to push it on a little bit more.'

From that moment we got off on a good foot. I felt courageous doing that because it was going to define our relationship. I was the new girl. It would have been easy for that to have gone wrong. It put me in that place of: 'You bought me. I'll do my best work for you but, equally, treat me as an adult.'

That's one that stands out for me. I felt a bit scared inside. Then I thought, 'Do you know what, I'm a 49-year-old woman. I've got three grown children. I don't have to work here.' And I think it was one of the first times that I put myself on the front foot. It was a defining point for me as well because generally I've been a 'please other people', 'be perfect' person. I love other people telling me I'm doing a wonderful job. But I thought, 'I have a chance in a new organisation to really be conscious about who I want to be.'

'What was driving that?' I wondered.
Evie answered:

A little bit of wisdom; thinking, 'I do know my stuff. She wants me to be successful. It's not going to look good on her if I'm not successful because she chose me.' My reading of her is that she wants strong people around her. Would she really want someone who was going to lie on their sword and go, 'I'm so sorry'? She's got hundreds of those around her but that isn't what she brought me in for. So, I tried to have that strength of conviction.

As well as challenging powerful individuals, I came across some powerful examples of individuals challenging the system. Priyanka, for example, acted to uphold an education institution's espoused values regarding diversity and social justice. She felt strongly that she needed to act on behalf of a student victim and the witnesses to what had happened. In doing so, Priyanka demonstrated fierce compassion. I admire her for taking a stand at considerable personal risk and for persevering through a long ordeal when it would have been easy to give up. She takes up the story:

My example was based around what was a pretty serious allegation by a student against a member of staff. I was pretty junior at the time. I was in some ways whistleblowing, which is always difficult on the individual. It's more difficult to take that risk when you are less stable in your career. I was untenured but I could not live with myself if I did not inform senior management that this had taken place; this was unacceptable. That was hard.

It also involved a lot of compassion to the student through supporting them through the system. Once you trigger a whistleblowing complaint at the university, you then have an investigation. In this case, it took almost a year. So, I escorted the student to all these meetings over the course of a year. I also felt very exposed because I was not tenured. I had taken the risk. I was being her voice and asking hard questions on her behalf. But I always felt very exposed doing that because I thought that this puts me at some risk as a professional.

In some ways, I question the wisdom of that because I think it still follows me around. I'm seen as somebody who agitates, who doesn't leave things alone. But I could not have lived with the decision of being silent. The outcome of the year-long investigation was not as satisfactory as I would have wanted. The staff member left, countersued the university and got a payoff. I did get the university to acknowledge that it did not fulfil its duty of care to the student and to mitigate the impact that it had on her degree. That in the end was successful. She graduated with a first.

It was a year-long saga of frustration because it was very slow. It was going against a system that was quite rigid in terms of thinking structurally about race and racism and what that meant. It had happened in a space where other students had seen it and had felt very angry, very disappointed, very outraged. And it was feeling like both an insider and outsider. I was an insider in that I was staff, but I was an outsider in that I was challenging the status quo.

Being a black person in higher education, I do a lot of diversity work. I thought, 'All this is pointless if we do not take the big things really seriously. There is no point having this entire work of diversity.' But also, for me, institutions of higher education are about social justice. So, we claim to try and make people's lives better. I think if we take this seriously, there are some things we absolutely should not do. We should try not to harm our students. We should try not to expose them to much worse racism than they might experience in other places. And so, that was what I couldn't leave.

In the following account, Nadia disputed the policies and practices of a national children's charity. Nadia's display of fierce compassion resulted in her becoming unpopular. However, she was able to bring about system-wide change:

There has been courage in my work life when I have challenged the way things are being done. That's been quite a painful experience because you seem to make powerful enemies.

In the late 1990s, in my role as a senior manager in a charity, I discovered that children with disabilities were being effectively locked up in some of their children's homes. The doors had double handles [one very high and one much lower] so a child with disabilities could not open their bedroom door and hence was locked in every night or if they went to their room during the day. The rationale was that it was for the child's own safety. The manager of the largest 'flagship' home explained that this system developed after a child had escaped and got out of the home.

I struggled with accepting this strategy because to me this was clearly abusive, but it was the policy of this very large influential charity and was accepted by everyone else. Challenging this took great courage, but after an internal struggle, I was unable to keep quiet in the face of my conviction. We needed to find other ways to keep the children safe.

Stopping the use of what was termed 'high handles' became a huge battle. It involved a rewrite of national policy, procedures and guidance and meant an increase in awake [as opposed to sleep-in] staff during the nights. This also meant increasing fees, which would result in decreasing occupancy and income for the charity. I particularly had a battle with my immediate managers and the manager of the flagship home.

I won the battle eventually as ultimately it could not be denied that the practice was abusive, and I received support from a national director. But in doing so, I was not forgiven by my immediate managers, with whom my relationship broke down irretrievably. I chose to leave afterwards.

The entire experience was extremely difficult for me personally. My immediate peer group of senior managers were supportive of me personally, albeit bemused by my perspective that this was a safeguarding issue and a matter of morality. All I could think about was what it must feel like to be a child locked up there.

I've had a few similar things in my career, which links to

feelings of compassion: being able to put yourself into other people's position and try and understand what they might be feeling. If it's not good enough for yourself, or your loved ones, then it is not good enough for others.

The final story in this chapter is an example of compassion fatigue. Sonja had tried to challenge and support a manager to do his job well, with little effect. Over time this had an adverse impact on her. Sonja decided to preserve her health and well-being, and leave the organisation without another job to go to. (Remember Leya?) She explained:

I've worked very hard to progress my career – crazy, long hours, really career driven. I kept getting this niggling feeling. I decided to quit my job in the spur of the moment. I was in this meeting and said, 'I just need to check in: are you all crazy, or am I? Because some days, I really don't know.' Everybody looked at me blankly. I explained. Someone had not done what he was supposed to do until the last minute and everybody was, 'You're amazing.' I'm thinking 'You're not amazing. Every week you tell us how shit you are at your job. And we're saying you're amazing.' I said, 'I'm done. I'm out.'

That took courage because it was that feeling in my tummy that this isn't right. This is an unhealthy situation. The conversations that following week took more courage. I had to think, 'What are the financial implications?' which were significant, and stick to that decision.

I allowed that compassion to really flow in: 'That isn't good for you. You could carry on earning all that money, but you need to be kind to yourself. You've been doing this for too long.' I think that gave me more courage. Letting compassion into myself is something I'm not very good at. So that was an unusual experience. I built on my wisdom from that situation.

I feel quite strongly about what the role of the manager is. This person was out to get praise for himself. I'd given him feedback directly to say, 'A lot of your team ask me questions that might indicate that you're not there enough for them. How could you support your team better? Is there any way we could support your team better?' I tried to coach this person towards doing a better job for his team. He didn't. So, when there was a European-wide meeting, and everybody was applauding this guy for doing something he should have done three months ago, it just broke me.

I knew I wasn't going to win, and I lost too much of my own energy. It was affecting my own health. I realised, 'It's not up to me to fix that situation.' And it's not part of my being to ignore it. It would eat away at me, and I have been deeply unhappy. I had to remove myself from that situation because I'd shown as much compassion as I could. Sometimes you can't fix the situation. It's too big. So, feeling helpless and that everything I was putting in wasn't impacting, but it was impacting me negatively. That's self-compassion.

Leading people through change

Leading people through change requires using the Three Companions if we want the change to be ultimately successful. Organisations undertake many initiatives that include changing the way that work is done, implementing new IT systems, creating a new capability framework, and shifting the focus from performance management to performance development. What I find interesting is that the people leading these projects sometimes underestimate or overlook the accompanying culture change, particularly for projects that do not fall into the transformation bucket.

Asking people to change is hard because we become accustomed to doing things a certain way. We have routines, we understand the unspoken rules, we know what is within our control, and so on. You may be familiar with the change curve (Samuel mentioned it in relation to his son, page 106), which plots the typical emotional journey of an individual undergoing change over time. We move from shock and denial to anger and despair before moving to acceptance. Courage, compassion and wisdom enable us to handle change sensitively. It requires courage to embark on the journey in the first place. When there are missteps, it also requires courage to admit the mistake rather than cover up. We need compassion to help people go through their change curve, support them to learn new ways of doing things or adapt to different roles or people, and wisdom to understand when to push and when to pull back and slow down.

The following stories are about the degree to which individuals called upon their Three Companions when leading change.

First, we meet Hans, who had to close and move a factory twice. He adopted two contrasting approaches: the first one fitted his leadership style, while the second was contrary to his preferred way of leading. Here, he describes them:

Factory closure 1:

I was running a business in Cambridge. I had joined after leaving college and worked my way up. I had to close it and move it to a different part of the country. I knew everybody in that business very well; some were close friends. It was very hard to move it from my hometown: not only was I leaving my family, but also shutting down the company that I've been very closely linked to for many years and all the people inside it.

I had to show courage because it was the right thing for the business, but it clearly wasn't the right thing for me. I had to think hard about the impact that was going to have on lots of people in a compassionate way. I had to show some wisdom and that I had the confidence to express the reason for doing that. Many people were looking to me to understand why we were making that decision.

There were about 130 people in that business at the time. I wanted to sit down with each of them, to communicate effectively, one to one, making sure that the information was clear for everybody and that I understood their situation. What did it really mean for them? What could we do to help them? What could we do differently? I tried to show compassion differently for different people for different reasons. Recognising that the situation for a couple of people was very different from someone who had a big family. That was an interesting journey because in that situation, you learn different things about people.

My role, as Operations Director, was to move the company from its current position to the South West [of England]. We'd acquired a competitor of ours. They had bigger premises there making the same products. It was a decision to 'lift and shift'.

I was young, indestructible, and more confident than I was wise. I don't think I had much wisdom at that point in my life, but enough to get by. It was focused on showing people some leadership in terms of direction and communication.

I started work when I was 13. So, I was used to working with manufacturing guys on the shop floor. That allowed me to understand people better. Those foundations enabled me to look at it from that perspective because it's all about the people.

Hans was a role model of how we would want to be in this type of immensely emotional situation. However, in the second factory closure, Hans felt that naivety played a part in how he handled the situation. At 28, he was drawing on the experience he had until that point. He reflected that he would respond differently today:

Factory closure 2:
I moved the company from Cambridge to Swindon, and then 14 months later we wanted to move that into another company that we'd acquired in the Midlands. So, I did it all again, which I found hard. I didn't have those personal connections and took a different approach. The previous process took six months, and we took people on a journey. This time, it was all done in secret; everyone was given their letters and told to go home on the Friday afternoon. Then I moved it over the weekend. On the Monday, the company was empty. It all moved up to the Midlands.

So that's when I didn't show compassion and be as courageous as I should have been. It was difficult, but because I'd been working with them for a small amount of time, it made it easier to do that. It made more sense to make it short and sharp. So, there were many conversations around, 'How would we do it? What would be the best way to do it?' We thought there would be a high risk of sabotage, a lack of productivity and massive disruption. That would be very difficult to manage in the marketplace.

There was clearly a big impact on a lot of people. They all lost their jobs. There were only a few people that moved. We made sure that we did the right thing. Financially, we didn't take any shortcuts because that would be immoral. The investment I had put into the previous one [factory closure] in terms of courage, compassion and wisdom was very different to this.

I asked, 'What made this harder for you than the first one?' Hans replied:

It was the people part. I knew that after a communication at 12:30 on a Friday, lots of families were going to be completely devastated. There's reading a letter, and then there's taking that letter home and explaining what's just happened to them. It was very hard to see people leaving, knowing that some of them weren't equipped to have the conversation that they needed to have with their loved ones.

I had a job to do. Ultimately, I also knew that we were building something even bigger in the Midlands. It was part of a bigger plan. Sometimes, you've got to take some smaller hits to build something much bigger. What kept me going was the confidence that it was the right business thing to do having gone through the scenarios, etc.

What struck me about this second story was that Hans still felt compassion for the people who were going to lose their jobs. His comfort was that it was the right business decision and that while these individuals were being adversely affected, there were others who would benefit from the company's growth. In situations where you cannot act in a way that is true to you, demonstrating self-compassion is helpful in accepting that internal conflict. It's also about treating people with dignity in the actions and communications that you can influence or control.

Samuel faced a similar situation; he had to close a business that had recently opened part of its operation in the Czech Republic:

Probably the biggest one [i.e. showing courage, compassion and wisdom] was deciding to close an entire business and move it to China, having been recently responsible for moving quite a significant amount of it to the Czech Republic. This was my first management role after finishing my graduate scheme.

It was a manufacturing company making parts for the automotive industry. I joined to run the UK part of the company. I had a team of about 100 people working for me, managing the distribution of parts to most of the UK-based car manufacturers. Part of my role had been to help move what had previously been parts that were manufactured in the United Kingdom to the Czech Republic.

I'd only been with the company about three or four months, but it was becoming incredibly apparent that moving it to the Czech Republic was one of the worst decisions the company could have ever made. You were asking a highly skilled workforce, who had never seen one of these antiquated machines, to run them cheaper than in the UK, where they had 15 years' experience. The wage bill now was different because the prospect of joining the EU meant that all the prices had gone up and inflation was rising. My candid view was, this is an absolute dog's dinner of a decision and the company's going to go bust if we allow it to keep going.

I knew that we had a small Chinese operation that was making some parts for the Chinese market with the

technology. And the car industry was offering big grants to companies that wanted to move manufacturing to China. I volunteered the idea and was asked to lead the transition, including the closure of a factory that we'd only just set up.

There's an argument to say it was un-compassionate to recommend shutting down something that you'd only just started up. You're talking about massive impacts on people's livelihoods and their families. But the people we were employing were not short of work. We were trying to get them to invest in skills that would be non-relevant to their wider economy. It felt more compassionate to call it quits quickly rather than to allow the situation to drag on.

My courage probably outweighed my wisdom because I was at a very early stage in my career. I was 23, 24. I was taking a big risk recommending it because I'd never closed a manufacturing network and moved it to China. Nor did I have the wisdom of how to do that. But I had enough knowledge of the situation to know it was clearly doomed.

Eleanor had founded and built a successful organisation. She decided it was time to step aside for a new CEO so that she could develop a new international offering. Her Board was behind her, and Eleanor naively thought that she could work alongside her successor. She did not anticipate or understand that he would feel threatened by her. It was a painful experience for her, as she was ousted from the organisation:

I'd been running the organisation for 12 years and reached the point where founder syndrome could become a problem. The organisation was successful but always had financial problems. It was clear the staff didn't have any more capacity for new strategic ideas. There was no new energy there. I thought I could shift and develop the international side and do a part-time position.

A year later, it was as clear as daylight that the new person couldn't stand it at all. He had to get rid of me. It had taken me courage to come out of a very stable and well-thought-of organisation. I then had to jump ship and set up my own independent consultancy. It was hugely painful, and I had very bad backaches consequently.

I was coming to the end of my career. In my head, I wasn't a threat to anyone else, but I obviously was. Before he got the job, I invited him to have supper with me. I thought we were getting on quite well. Then he said, 'So why? You really think that we're going to work together? You don't think this could possibly work?' I was absolutely floored. I couldn't believe that somebody would take that position at the very beginning. It was very naive of me.

On our first day, after several hours of handover, he said, 'This is not going to work.'

I said, 'What are you talking about?'

He said, 'This is not going to work. You know everything and I know nothing. I'm not going to be able to do this.'

I burst into tears. I felt sorry for myself because he wasn't understanding me. It was clear he did not like me. He didn't want me to be there. He felt extremely threatened. Very quickly I got a huge international contract and that was the way he got rid of me. He set up a committee that was looking at risk. He brought me into a meeting, and they said, 'This is risky; we don't think that we should be taking this on.'

That was just horrendous. I thought I was being wise in putting forward this idea and my Board had supported me. I thought that it would be easy to do it because I was good at working with people. So, I wasn't wise in understanding that other people couldn't cope with it.

What do you do when a member of an all-volunteer team you are in, is antagonistic and rejects all your attempts to collaborate? This is the situation that Roger faced when he was elected to the Board of a charity with a brief to bring big, positive changes to transform a part of the organisation, but a long-standing volunteer team member was hostile towards him:

I remember the moment I got this email throwing dolls out of the pram. I had just completed a challenging assignment in Cyprus when the email landed. I spent three or four hours trying to construct a response, which wasn't a 'fuck you' response. I did eventually manage to construct that.

That was difficult for me because I was trapped. I had taken on that voluntary position without knowing what I was inheriting. It required a great deal of staying power. It troubled me enormously because he [the team member] couldn't engage. I tried to speak on the phone, and we tried to meet in person. I never understood what was going on for him. He was carrying a lot of baggage, having worked hard for the previous years and that not being recognised. So, I had to hang in there. I nearly resigned. I thought, 'This is too unpleasant and difficult.' And I'm delighted that I didn't. I was supported by one or two people on the global Board who would listen to me for a long time and give me wise counsel.

I faced down that dynamic and that individual, plus other people who were associated with that person. I felt a compassion for the endeavour. I put a lot of effort into not lashing out at that individual, who was being unreasonable. He couldn't engage in any kind of sensible conversation but had passwords and bank details, so all the power was in his hands.

A lot of courage came into this and holding that intention to do what I believed was right. He didn't accept my authority. When I would thank him for something, he would get furious. So, every single interaction became problematic.

184

I commented, 'I'm wondering to what extent there was compassion towards him and towards yourself?'

Roger explained:

I would say towards him there was a little bit buried under quite a lot of irritation. After he resigned, I asked a trusted individual, 'This is unfinished business. Would you be willing to have a three-way meeting?' He said he would ask that person. The person said, 'No, there's nothing to talk about.' So that effectively closed the door.

I can still feel it. I don't think I showed any compassion for him, but I was resolved not to inflame the situation. I had to work hard at being measured and reasonable. I was trying to be collaborative across the whole piece. My attempts at collaboration appeared to be very provocative. So, I was enormously patient, and courageous, but I suffered.

Evie's next story took place much earlier in her career than her previous one (see page 170). Her role was to lead the people workstream to set up a new facility in Russia. Evie utilised her Three Companions to successfully get a factory up and running, with motivated staff, in a culture she was unfamiliar with. She describes what happened:

When I was doing a regional HR role, we built a new facility in Russia. I went out and got to know the people there. We built the team. I was going in and out of Russia. It was a new experience. It wasn't a comfortable culture for me. Whereas some other cultures, I embraced more easily.

I needed a lot of courage to think, 'I need to set the scene for this people workstream. I need to make it feel comfortable and confident, with absolutely no idea what I need to do.' I think from a compassion point of view, I had a lot to understand, including bringing a group of people in Russia into the way of a global company. Equally, recognising that there was a push from the global lead about not getting it wrong and mitigating risk.

From a wisdom point of view, it was finding the voices to listen to. Also, some intuition to trust my own judgement. So, thinking, 'When you've run a project before, what is it you need to do?' When you try to make people feel confident in a vision, even if it's not completely right, you have still got to give people a map, be bold and do it.

I've pulled on that experience many times when I've had a moment of like, 'Oh! OK, where do you start? Well, I helped build a facility in Russia from scratch. Come on, anything's possible.'

I hope you have been inspired by reading these stories. We are all human. Human beings are imperfect. We are not going to use model behaviours in every instance – and that's OK. My hope is that these stories resonate with you and you either feel confirmed in what you do now, or you feel encouraged to make some changes that will lead to more rewarding outcomes.

In Part Three, we will look at how you can grow your own courage, compassion and wisdom.

3
DEVELOPING COURAGE, COMPASSION AND WISDOM

This final part of the book is designed to help you determine how you can recognise and develop your Three Companions. There are two parts to this:

- A five-step development process that you can follow or tailor to suit your own style of learning (see page 191).
- A description of supportive practices in five key domains that will help you to use the Three Companions (see page 199).

In developing any competency, we move through four stages as shown in the following diagram:

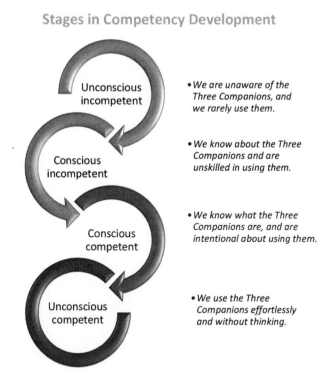

Stages in Competency Development

Unconscious incompetent
- *We are unaware of the Three Companions, and we rarely use them.*

Conscious incompetent
- *We know about the Three Companions and are unskilled in using them.*

Conscious competent
- *We know what the Three Companions are, and are intentional about using them.*

Unconscious competent
- *We use the Three Companions effortlessly and without thinking.*

Think about which stage you are in currently and where you want to get to. (I think I hover between conscious incompetent and conscious competent.) A factor that helps us develop our Three Companions is knowing how to recognise the associated behaviours. This is the reason for providing you with the examples in Part Two. You can see how the Three Companions show up in different circumstances, and once you recognise the behaviours associated with using the Three Companions, you can start to discern them in yourself.

The supportive practices are routines relating to specific domains that I believe support our use of the Three Companions. My hypothesis was confirmed by my interviewees.

My advice is to choose only one or two domains that you want to strengthen initially. This is because behaviour change takes concerted effort and time. Once you have mastered these, you can revisit this process and determine one or two new domains to enhance.

How to grow your Three Companions

The five-step development process is a guide to help you determine the steps that you could take to reveal and grow your Three Companions. I have included examples of what this looks like for me.

Step 1: Where do you want to be?

The first step is to visualise how you want to embody the Three Companions. When you are at your best, how do you want to exhibit courage, compassion, and wisdom? In what settings? With whom? This is your aspiration; in an ideal world, this is how you would like to be.

Use your imagination

A lovely technique to try here is to close your eyes and imagine yourself displaying the Three Companions in your ideal way. Then to use your five senses to create a more tangible vision:

- *What do you see?* Think about the environment you are in, the people you are with, how you look, what you are doing, what others are doing.
- *What do you hear?* Conjure up the sounds in your vision; for example, music, conversation, laughter, nature, machines, traffic.
- *What can you taste?* This can be food or drink, or even a state of being, such as the taste of success.
- *What can you smell?* Perhaps you can smell flowers, cut grass, coffee, perfume or fresh laundry?

- *What can you touch?* This can relate to your environment – the feel of a chair, an object you are holding, etc.; or it could be the sense of an emotion such as love, happiness, grief or sadness.

This is your vision, so take your time to imagine it and then capture the essential points in whatever form works best for you – recording, handwritten note, Word document and so forth.

After you have done this, take a break and leave this for at least 30 minutes. Return to your vision and see how it makes you feel. If you feel excited and energised, you know you are on the right path. It can also feel daunting at this point. If it does not grab you, it is not quite right. In this case, I suggest you repeat the visualisation exercise until you feel energised by what you envisage.

My own vision

My vision for how I display my Three Companions is that in every interaction that I have, I am thinking about the dynamic between us and I can tune in to what we both need in each moment. I act in a way that is consistent with that by doing or saying the right thing. This is not necessarily the easy thing. In fact, it is often difficult, and I face into the challenge, rather than shy away from it. When I get this wrong, and one or other of us feels worse from our interaction, I learn from it.

I see myself in different settings with people: friends, family, groups, individual conversations, at work, on holiday, at home. In each one, I am making meaningful contact. I can see this in the connection we make. I am touched by the people I am with, physically and emotionally. I hear voices and the sound of silence. I smell whatever environment we are in and I taste delicious food and drink.

Use images

Another powerful method is to use pictures. You can either use picture cards or go onto a website that allows you to download photos at no charge, for example, Pexels and Unsplash. [17, 18]

- This exercise is best done with a partner, someone who can help you to clarify your vision.
- Scroll or flick through the images and stop when you find one that you are drawn to.
- Describe to your partner what it is that attracts you to this image.
- Your partner asks you questions to draw out different aspects of the image. For example, you may notice a light shining through some trees that represents your enlightened state of being when you are using your Three Companions. A stretch of water may represent the calm way that you engage with others.
- Notice different textures and tones, shade, colour, how busy the image is, and so on.
- Reflect on how these relate to your aspirations in using the Three Companions.
- Once you have exhausted the image, you can choose to download it as a reminder.
- Then continue scrolling until you find another image that resonates with you.
- Repeat the process as before. What extra insights have you got with this second picture?

Step 2: Where are you now?

It is important for you to get a handle on how you currently use the Three Companions. You can refer to the stories in Part Two to help you assess what you do in different situations.

For example, someone close to you may be seriously ill. How are you using the Three Companions to cope with this? You could look at stories in the chapter 'Coping with illness' to see how your response compares to these. There is no right or wrong way. This is to give you an idea of what you do well and those domains where you might want to do more.

How I use the Three Companions

I use my Three Companions variably. In my work as a consultant and coach, I use them well by intentionally creating safe spaces for individuals to explore their truth. I need to be courageous to provide challenging feedback and difficult messages. I consider what the best way is to be with my clients to create a positive impact and to share my truth. I also facilitate groups where the purpose is to connect, share and learn.

Where I'm less good is situations in my personal life, where a conversation can turn in an unexpected direction and my response is based on emotions other than the Three Companions. I can tell this because I dwell on what happened and what I did that was far from my ideal. Over the past year I have learnt to exercise self-compassion, so I do not beat myself up for too long. I have room to grow here.

The stories that resonated with my aspiration were from Elin (page 55), Emma (page 73), Niamh (pages 76 and 94), Saskia (page 77 and 96). Elin shared her fantasies with a counsellor, who helped her normalise and recognise her experience. This enabled her to notice her negative thoughts and desires, accept them, and take away the power that they had. Instead of judging, Emma was a loving presence for her friend. She allowed him to be himself by accepting him unconditionally. Niamh managed her own emotions so that she could see the bigger picture and the needs of her son. Saskia expressed her love and belief in her daughter. She also learnt from a regret that she needed to have courage to face her fear of death.

From this I take away three behaviours to try:

1. To draw on my empathy to focus on the needs of the other person more often.
2. Accept and normalise the times when I don't use my Three Companions.
3. Learn from my missteps by reflecting in a constructive way (not ruminate) to determine what to change for next time.

Step 3: Identify areas to strengthen

The first step was to create a vision and the second was about identifying where you are currently when it comes to the Three Companions. Now you will be setting a goal that will take you towards realising your vision. My experience of working with leaders and individuals on four continents – Africa, Asia-Pacific, Americas, Europe – is that we focus primarily on a deficit model. *What are my gaps? How can I close them?* In addition to our default position of looking at limitations, I think that we should consider building up our strengths further.

In this respect, I think we need to work on two levels. The first is to identify the behaviours to try that will help us to realise our vision. You can do this by analysing what the individual does in the stories that you like. Alternatively, you can identify people who display the qualities that you want to enhance and elucidate what they do. In my example, I have realised that I use my Three Companions at work and want to understand how I do that to see how much of that I can transfer to my personal life.

The second level is to assess where you stand in relation to the five domains (see page 199) that help us to reveal our Three Companions.

In my case, I have identified self-compassion as an area that I want to continue improving.

> ## My goals
> I want to learn from what I do in my work situations so that I can apply these lessons in my personal life. My goals are therefore to:
>
> - Strengthen my practice of self-compassion
> - Understand the difference between what I do in my work and personal settings so that I can improve my use of my Three Companions in the latter

Step 4: Act

To achieve our goal, we need to act! When making behavioural changes, it may feel clumsy and we may not get it right at first. However, with perseverance, we will improve and move from *conscious incompetent* to *conscious competent* and eventually to *unconscious competent*, as shown in the diagram on page 189. If we take a learning approach to this, we can experiment with new behaviours and observe how effective these are (or get feedback on this). With this experience, we can adjust what we do subsequently.

Some of you may like to have a structured approach to this, in which case a plan may help you. The plan could include:

- Your goal
- How you will measure progress; for example, how you feel, what others say
- Steps you are going to take; for example, identify specific situations, rehearse conversations, practice mindfulness, observe others
- Support that you need, and from whom
- Obstacles that may get in your way and how you will overcome these

I find that going through the steps of creating a plan helps me to structure my thoughts. That's enough to get me started, and I do not need to refer to this plan on an ongoing basis. I can hold myself to account for what I commit to. You may be like me and will dedicate time and energy to realising your goal. Or you may need to have an accountability partner to keep you on track. You need to know what works best for you to ensure that you act.

Step 5: Review and refine

When you have experimented with some different behaviours, it is worthwhile contemplating your experience and what you notice. *How did it feel? What was the impact on you and others? How effective were you? What did you or others observe?* And so on.

The purpose of this reflective practice is to create the opportunity for you to take stock of how you are using your Three Companions compared to what you set out to achieve, and either to continue along the path you have chosen or refine your behaviours in order to try something a little different. This is an iterative process that helps you deepen your learning and strengthen your skills.

When you are satisfied with your progress, you can determine whether you want to set a new goal.

You may recognise this as a classic behavioural change process. Remember, this is one idea of how you might enhance your use of the Three Companions. I invite you to develop an approach that is true to you.

Five domains to support the use of the Three Companions

I analysed my interviewees' stories to see if there were any characteristics whose presence or absence impacted their ability to use the Three Companions. Five domains emerged that were present in most stories. These factors were:

- Self-compassion
- Personal values
- Personal boundaries
- Self-care
- Support network

I tested my hypothesis with my interviewees to see whether they recognised these as helpful. They confirmed my proposition that the supportive practices in these five domains do indeed help us to manifest our Three Companions, and we will be looking at these in more detail in this chapter – from exercising self-compassion to the importance of having a support network in place.

Self-compassion, self-care and finding the right support for our needs were hard for many of my interviewees to invoke. I believe one of the reasons for this is that we are brought up to be selfless; to think of others, take care of their needs, share what we have. A message that I and many others have internalised is that it is bad to be self-centred. This makes it hard to engage in activities that are nurturing of ourselves.

However, when we do practise self-compassion, self-care and have an effective support network in place, we become stronger, more resilient and empowered. Feeling more resourced, we are better able to use our Three Companions to help others.

Trust was a significant emotion that enabled some of my interviewees to use their Three Companions. This was trust in themselves and believing that they were doing the right thing. Conversely, when individuals experienced self-doubt or judged themselves to fall short, they were not able to use courage, compassion and wisdom. I mentioned in Part Two that fear often showed up in the stories. On occasion this did hamper individuals from expressing their Three Companions. This was fear of how they would be seen by others or fear of saying or doing the wrong thing. A couple of people said that shame was a hindrance for them. The shame was related to not fitting into society's perceived norms or not living up to their own standards of how they wanted to be.

Reflecting on their experiences helped my interviewees to gain new insights about themselves. I saw this during the interviews themselves. For example, Idris and Faith did not appreciate that they were using their Three Companions until we had the discussion and they learnt how to recognise them.

Prior to finalising the text for this book, I asked each person to review their stories and what helped or hindered them from using their Three Companions. This process afforded another chance for reflection on their experience. Seeing their story in print evoked a range of emotions in them; I detected pride, excitement, gratitude, delight and vulnerability. A few were pleasantly surprised at the person they saw reflected in the story; they did not recognise themselves. I also heard that contemplating which of the practices were present took some of them back to the emotions they felt at the time of the event.

In the CCW Community we share our views and experiences of different topics, such as: 'When is it appropriate to speak your truth?', 'Coping strategies for unexpected life changes', and 'Using courage, compassion, and wisdom when we receive unsolicited advice'. We learn from the different perspectives and experiences and that deepens our understanding of what the Three Companions mean and what helps or hinders us.

We are unique individuals, so the 'recipe' that enables each of us to reveal our Three Companions when we need them will be distinctive to us. There is no magic formula that we can apply; it very much depends on the situation. Sofia and Camila felt no need to exercise self-compassion or self-care in their stories about helping a colleague back to work (see page 79) or handling the crisis in London (page 111), respectively. And Hannah didn't practise self-care or turn to others for support when she chose to act normally with her friend with breast cancer (page 72). Contrast this with Faith, who used her Three Companions to help her stand firm in her belief about the best way to support her daughter (page 61). Or Hugo, who employed the Three Companions to speed up his healing by leaving his monkship (page 165); while Phyllis engaged her courage, compassion and wisdom in how she used her breast cancer to generate benefits for others (page 65).

My interpretation of this distinction is that we have a nuanced relationship with the five domains that help us express the Three Companions. When we are using our Three Companions to face a personal challenge, we are more likely to require all five to help ourselves through than when we are supporting another through their difficulties. This means that in developing your Three Companions, you need to consider the context and situations that you are facing: what is your role? Once you have determined this, you can identify which of the five domains will be most beneficial to you.

In the rest of this chapter, I provide a detailed description of each of the five domains and some ideas about how you can develop them. I offer these to you so that you can consider your own tendencies and determine what changes you want to make. For each domain consider:

1. How strong am I in this domain?
2. When do I employ the supportive practices for this domain? How might I use this knowledge to help me in times where I don't?

3. What aspects could I strengthen?
4. What action will I take?
5. How will I review progress?

I will be inviting you to look at each of the five domains in turn.

The domain that I choose to work on

The domain I need to work on relates to maintaining my personal boundaries. I realise that these get compromised when I am unhappy and feel there is a significant risk to me if I express my feelings. In my professional role, I know where my limits are and will express that to my clients. However, in personal situations I worry about damaging the relationship.

When I am supporting others, I know how far I can go in providing that help. I am playing a different role than when I am the focus of using my Three Companions. I think this is where self-compassion can help me to develop my practice of reinforcing my boundaries; I need to be in that supportive role to myself.

So, one action I can take is to reflect on how I would support others in similar situations.

I will know that I am making progress when I have fewer moments of angst in expressing what I want.

Self-compassion

As already stated when describing compassion on page 23, compassion means 'to suffer with', and comes from the Latin *com*, meaning 'with', and *pati*, meaning 'to suffer'. It is a feeling of sorrow or tenderness for someone who is suffering or experiencing misfortune. It requires an individual to notice the suffering of another and to want that to be alleviated either by themselves or others. This can be through offering them kindness and understanding rather than criticism and judgement when they fail, make mistakes or take missteps.

Self-compassion is when you offer that kindness and understanding to yourself at those moments when you are having a difficult time. For example, you make a mistake or notice something that you don't like about yourself, but instead of being self-critical, you act as your own best friend and accept yourself unconditionally. You have the humility to admit your strengths and limitations, and recognise that you do not need to be perfect. You appreciate that things will not always go the way that you want; you will make mistakes, experience frustrations and disappointments, fall short of your ideals, and so forth.

Why is it important to have self-compassion? Research shows that self-compassion provides numerous benefits to health and well-being, including reduced anxiety and depression, a source of empowerment, inner strength and increased resilience.[19] The more you can recognise that things not going how you would like them to is part of being human, the easier it is to show yourself compassion.

Dr Kristin Neff, an associate professor at the University of Texas, describes self-compassion as comprising three elements:

- Self-kindness
- Common humanity
- Mindfulness[20]

Let's look at these three aspects in turn, before considering how we can develop self-compassion through a range of reflective practices.

Self-kindness

A natural tendency when we feel inadequate, insecure or fail – i.e., when we are suffering – is to judge ourselves negatively and be self-critical. This is self-defeating since we respond to criticism with a range of emotions such as defensiveness, humiliation, anger, devastation and disappointment. Our brain does not distinguish between criticism meted out by others or ourselves.

Self-kindness is about showing understanding, sensitivity, and benevolence to ourselves. It is about recognising that we are as deserving of care and concern as everyone else.

Common humanity

We often feel that we are alone in our particular situation of distress. We believe that no one will comprehend what we are going through and that our problems are unique. Self-compassion recognises that suffering is part of the human condition. Many people have experienced similar circumstances to the very ones that we feel are exceptional. Recognising this is often accompanied by a sense of relief and a feeling of 'we are not alone'.

Mindfulness

Mindfulness in self-compassion requires us to take a balanced approach to our negative feelings so that we neither suppress them nor exaggerate them. When we quash what we deem to be negative emotions, we are not able to show compassion for ourselves and the pain we feel. Over-amplifying our emotions means that we get caught up in our negative thoughts and ruminate, which increases our suffering. Mindfulness allows us to notice and observe ourselves with non-judgement. We are open to and curious about our negative thoughts and feelings.

Self-compassion gives us the emotional safety to turn towards our pain and has been linked to enhanced intra- and interpersonal well-being.[21] Self-compassion is a resource that is available to us in good times and bad. By combining mindful acceptance of our present-moment experience with the compassionate desire to be happy and free from suffering, we maximise our ability to heal and reach our full potential.

Fortunately, the skills of self-compassion can be learnt and maintained over time, and there are various activities that can help us with this – from journaling to joining like-minded communities.[22]

Journaling

Write down your uncensored thoughts to get your negative talk out of your head. I find keeping a journal useful because it has stopped me from ruminating. I write in my journal as part of my morning ritual before I start my day. You may prefer to journal in the evening so that you can reflect on your day. I rarely revisit what I have written. It is enough for me to write. Others like to review and process what they have written to make sense of it. I write in a notebook using a special pen; this adds to my experience. You may prefer to make notes on your laptop. Choose a medium that suits you.

Meditating

There are many guided meditations and apps available for you to experiment with. I think with guided meditation, the voice is important. Take time to listen to a few voices to see which resonate with you. The length of time that people meditate varies from a few minutes to an hour or longer. I find that if you are not a practised meditator, it helps to build up the length of time at your own pace until you find a duration that is right for you. There are general meditations and focused ones. I move between a general meditation and one designed for self-compassion. You may prefer to meditate without the aid of someone to lead you through the steps. I encourage you to experiment to see what works for you. It's a personal choice.

Be your best friend

When you notice that you are beating yourself up, stop and think about what you would say to your best friend if they were in a similar position. Apply that advice to yourself.

Write yourself a love letter

Harness your best friend quality to write yourself a love letter that reminds you of all the wonderful attributes you have, what you have accomplished, and what you bring to the world. Tell yourself that you have the resources and capabilities to get through whatever challenges you. Pour your love into this letter and keep it somewhere prominent so that you can refer to it often.

(Self-)compassion programme

Many organisations offer programmes on compassion in which there is a component of self-compassion. For example, the Compassion Institute runs several programmes designed to cultivate compassion.[23] I completed their flagship Compassion Cultivation Training, which greatly improved my meditation practice.

Join or create a community

One of the powerful learnings from participating in the CCW Community has been our common humanity. We have felt a range of shared emotions during the pandemic, such as anxiety, anger, hope, sadness, grief, joy, and many more. We have languished, been motivated, dreaded winter, felt uplifted by spring – and so forth. What we realised is that we are not alone in what we encounter. The CCW Community helped us to normalise our experiences and learn various ways of coping with our emotions and different situations. The CCW Community helped to increase our self-compassion and resilience. There are also other communities that you can join, which will help you to process your emotions in a safe way and help you build your self-compassion practice.

Several of my interviewees reported finding it easier to show compassion to others than to themselves. Kristin Neff and Chris Germer, who co-designed the 'Mindful Self-Compassion' programme, cited research at a Compassion in Therapy Summit which shows that if you intentionally develop self-compassion, you will also increase your compassion for others.[24] It's like the announcement they make on the airplane safety briefing: 'Fit your own oxygen mask before helping others.' Compassion for others increases self-compassion, and self-compassion increases compassion for others. Chris Germer states, 'In Buddhist psychology, compassion for oneself is really considered the foundation of compassion for others.'[25] In their programme they start with how we treat others as a basis for learning how to be compassionate towards ourselves.

Self-compassion can be expressed in various ways. For example, while courting his wife-to-be, Hugo learnt that she experienced symptoms of depression. He also knew that he too could experience depressive symptoms. He tended to judge these in himself and felt he would be at risk of judging them in his wife too. So, he chose to see her behaviour as a reminder for him to give compassion both to her and to himself:

I entered into our relationship with a clear intent to notice any judgements I felt about my wife. I would treat my judgements as reminders to give compassion to the vulnerable parts of my wife and to mine too. I get so much from her because of her love. The compassion and joy that we share in companionship are immense.

Demonstrating self-compassion requires us to be in tune with ourselves and notice how we respond to negative events. In the discussions of the CCW Community, we revisited self-compassion frequently as a way of coping during difficult times. I believe self-compassion is the cornerstone of enabling us to use our Three Companions, particularly when we are the ones who are suffering.

Personal values

There are many personal characteristics that influence what we do: skills, knowledge, self-image, traits, motives and values. These attributes exist at different levels of consciousness. Personal values are those principles or standards of behaviour that we deem to be important to us. They drive our behaviour and how we engage with others. We are somewhat conscious of them, and other people may detect them from our behaviour patterns. They are specific to us and are derived from a number of influences in our lives.

Personal values are often formed based on what we have learnt in our social conditioning – from our parents, teachers, friends, family members, religion, our leaders, or work. For example, if our work emphasises teamwork and collaboration, we will likely make an effort to involve others in our work and volunteer to be part of project teams even when our preference is to work quietly on our own. We know this is important if we want to be successful. Or, if our parents believe that family comes first, our values mean that we will probably attend family events and drop everything to rally round in times of trouble, even if it comes at a personal cost.

Often the values that we live by are not what really energises us; for example, our values may mean that we believe we should perform well in our academic studies, or we need to extend help to everyone who asks, or we should respect our elders and not challenge them – but we may need external reinforcement to remind us that these are important codes of behaviour. They are obligations that we believe we have little choice over. In the absence of this reinforcement, we will gravitate to what we enjoy; activities that give us a buzz and are self-sustaining.

This is neither good nor bad. We all experience times when we have to expend energy doing things that we would rather not. We may have adopted values from our parents, and other significant people in our lives, without questioning them and what they mean to us. This is fine until we have a negative response to someone without understanding why. Something feels off. In the conversations that I had, values impacted whether individuals were able to show courage, compassion and wisdom or not. When they dug deeper, they realised that either they were acting against their own values, or the person they were interacting with was behaving in a way that violated their code of conduct.

Below, I illustrate this point with a couple of examples that we have previously encountered in Part Two. Here, we are looking at them through the lens of values:

- Rose (see page 156) was offended by the objectification of women. My interpretation that the value being violated here was *dignity*. She described feeling contempt emanating from him as he showed her the picture in the newspaper.
- Leya (see page 63) realised that her absence of the Three Companions was because her sister did not take *personal responsibility*.

Both these stories and many others highlight how our values can influence us in ways that we may not fully appreciate in the moment.

There are several exercises that can help you to identify what your values are, which you will find described below.

Reflection

When we feel emotions such as resentment, outrage or indignation, it is worth noticing this and enquiring into this in order to understand what is provoking that response. You could start by asking yourself: *When do I feel this way? What am I doing? Who am I with? What am I thinking? What happened? Why do I feel this way?*

Think about what you believe is important and whether these beliefs are being impacted. You may find it easier to talk through the situation with a trusted friend who can listen out for your values.

Left side, right side

The 'left side, right side' exercise allows us to analyse an interaction by separating out the dialogue from the thoughts and feelings that arose. Essentially, you divide your paper (physical or virtual) in two by drawing a vertical line. On the left-hand side, write down the dialogue as you remember it. Once you have completed that, go back to the start and in the right-hand column, note down the thoughts and feelings that you had in relation to what was being said. Note at what point your negative feelings, e.g., frustration, anger, were activated and examine what provoked these emotions. Again, consider which of your values might have been triggered.

Value cards

Value cards are readily available. These are packs of cards with value words written on them. (Some packs have pictures to represent the values.) Go through the pack and create two or three piles: 'keep', 'reject', 'maybe'. Push away the 'reject' pile. Go through the cards in the two remaining piles and sort into 'keep' and 'reject'. Finally, go through the 'keep' pile and reduce this number to up to five values that matter most to you.

When you have identified the patterns associated with your values being violated, either by yourself or others, you are in a better position to notice what is happening in the moment. This gives you increased choice about how you want to continue the conversation. It depends on what importance you place on using your Three Companions. If you are striving to display these virtues in most, or all, of your interactions with others, this will elevate their importance to you. In those difficult moments when another value is compromised, you can pause and choose the Three Companions above that value.

For example, if gratitude is important to you, and someone turns on you because they are upset, your instinct might be to withdraw because they are not showing gratitude towards you. In that moment, if you remind yourself that your Three Companions are more important, this will help you to continue to provide a compassionate presence despite feeling hurt.

If you have values of dignity and respect, you may not tolerate the person lashing out at you. In this case, you can politely and firmly let the individual know that their behaviour is not acceptable.

This is still a display of the Three Companions because you are choosing to tell the individual how you feel, which can take courage. The compassion here is in the form of fierce compassion (acting against injustice) and the wisdom lies in speaking out, so the individual understands that there is a boundary that they should not cross.[26]

Personal boundaries

Another factor that seems to influence how readily we can reveal our Three Companions involves our personal boundaries. My observation is that when we reach these limits, or they are crossed, we are hampered in our ability to use our Three Companions in our interactions with others. The opportunity then is discerning what our boundaries are and how we know that they are being tested in the moment, rather than, as is more often the case, after that line has been crossed and it is too late.

It is important to have personal boundaries in place so that we can have healthy relationships with others. They are the guidelines, rules or limits that we create to identify reasonable, safe and permissible ways for other people to behave towards us. Also, it is about how we respond when someone steps over those boundaries and the consequences that we impose. We may not know exactly what our personal boundaries are, but we tend to know what it feels like when someone tramples over them. Denise was indignant that her friend showed no respect for her boundaries (see page 116). Isla felt that she had been pushed too far by her friend (see page 118).

Setting boundaries is a way of caring for ourselves. It does not mean we are selfish or unfeeling because we don't always do things in the way that others want us to. Boundaries allow us to communicate our needs and desires clearly and succinctly. They allow us to set limits so that others don't take advantage of or hurt us. Setting boundaries enables us to practise self-care and self-respect. As I have stated previously, maintaining my boundaries is a challenge for me in some circumstances. One manifestation of this relates to receiving unsolicited advice.

When other people give me advice, I am grateful for this when I ask for it or if someone has helped me to have an insight that enables me to figure out how I might resolve the situation for myself. This can be in my relationships, my health, or how to perform a piece of work. The key point here is that I am supported to conclude or decide for myself. However, if someone imposes their view on me, even if it is coming from a good place with positive intent, I can rail against it. This can lead to a range of emotions, including judgement, indignation and dismay. A boundary has been crossed and I shut down. In that moment I am unable to draw on my Three Companions. I react rather than respond. I cannot acknowledge the positive intent or concern from the other person or assert myself and make it clear that this is a boundary issue for me.

With unhealthy boundaries we lose our dignity, self-respect and self-esteem, as we may find ourselves going against our values to please others. We keep giving of ourselves and may feel that our own needs are ignored. When we allow others to determine what we like, where we are going, or who we are, we are allowing them to control us. This is a sign that we have unhealthy boundaries. Another type of unhealthy boundary is expecting others to fill our needs; for example, to make us happy, or be responsible for the way our life is.

Ria is a gentle and kind person who had unhealthy boundaries. She took on the suffering of others to the extent that it incapacitated her. She explains:

> I can have compassion where people tell me problems. Often what happens is, I'm oversensitive so then it hurts me too much. I think the whole time about their problems, and I forget to do what I have to do. I forget to prepare a meal or think about a problem that a relative has who I'm committed to helping. It takes over and that's not good because the person doesn't benefit from that.

Although it was hard, Ria learnt to set boundaries by questioning whether she could help. She realised she desperately wanted the other person to change and that this was driving her act. Recognising this enabled her to step back. This distance allowed her to see situations more clearly.

Arthur is the director of an institute that conducts research in and provides education on compassion. In our interview, he was emphatic that we need to have the resources to give but not at the expense of our well-being. He put it this way: 'The fact that they needed something, sometimes is irrelevant. The question is, "What do you need?" You can't sacrifice your own comfort and self in the hopes that you're going to make someone else happy. That's not always an effective strategy for self-care.' He is willing to do what he can to help someone in need. However, Arthur is clear that he has limits and will not accept full responsibility for helping another person when they have other people who could also support them. His feelings echo those of Roger (see page 136). Arthur told me:

> Why am I even put in that position when he has family? He has resources. I have done as much as I feel comfortable with, and as much as I can without impacting myself in a negative way. It is unfair to me to ask me to sacrifice my own well-being when he has a significant number of other resources. I have maxed out my own capacity and I won't allow myself to feel bad about it. That is my boundary, and I won't cross it. I do wish him the best, but it is all I can do.

Casey is a spiritual healer in a small town in the USA. Her example of not using the Three Companions was due to not setting boundaries with her staff. She believes, 'It takes a lot of courage, compassion, and wisdom to be able to have good boundaries.' That's an interesting perspective since I believe the reverse is true and can see that there might be a symbiotic relationship between the Three Companions and having good boundaries.

Casey sometimes employed students, clients and friends who understood the services she was offering and could take bookings for her, for example. This blurred the lines between them being employees and having another type of relationship with her. Yet Casey felt dependent on them because she was a solo entrepreneur. She recognised that, 'I put up with a lot because I wanted to be the nice guy and be more spiritual. I didn't do boundaries soon enough.' The reason she cites for not doing so was:

> Fear of failure or fear of not having somebody help me do the work. I had so much on my plate that I thought I couldn't do this without the help of somebody. So, I think fear of not being able to do my work without having someone.

Manon learnt the hard way to establish some criteria and boundaries for the clients she was willing to accept on her platform. Due to her sense of fairness, Manon denied what her wisdom was telling her. She said:

> I had a conversation with a client last week; she was so negative, unfairly so. I'm very sensitive to those comments. I knew it was going to be a difficult conversation because from the very first moment she joined the platform, she was quite hostile. So, when we had this conversation lined up, I thought there must be something going on for her that's causing this. I went into that call with a sense of curiosity. I wanted to find out, 'What can I do to help?' But it was just a verbal attack.
>
> I was trying to show compassion and came away with wisdom. I should have followed my intuition from the word go.
>
> Before I set up the platform, my supervisor said, 'What happens if somebody wants to come on the platform and you don't like them?'

I said, 'I find it difficult that I wouldn't like a client, we're a lovely community. If I set the criteria, I must abide by them. If they tick all the boxes, then I can't turn somebody away just because I don't like their attitude.' But maybe I need to build something else into the criteria about the kind of person they are.

Having that sort of clarity helps us to navigate tricky situations. I tie myself in knots about how fair am I being with my boundaries. What is my justification for drawing that line? I need to turn to my support network to test whether I am being reasonable. Even when my friends agree with my position, I still find myself wobbling at the thought of a robust challenge. In those situations, I desert my Three Companions. The result is that I tend to be very accommodating until you cross an invisible line and then I am resolute in writing people off. I need to find a place in the middle that allows me to access that edginess to remain firm while enforcing my boundaries so that I can retain the relationship.

Setting and reinforcing boundaries

How do we ensure that the boundary is there to maintain the balance between our needs and helping others, rather than to be self-serving and an excuse not to do anything?

Not an easy question to answer. I think we need to enquire within: what is our motivation? Do we want to help and can we? Have we already tried? What is our experience with this person? What have we encountered in similar situations? What impact did it have on us?

How do we set and reinforce our boundaries? The first thing is to spend time thinking about potentially problematic areas, as per the list below,[27] and how we want to relate to individuals in these. You may think of others that are more relevant to you:

- *Money:* **How much money (if any) will you lend and to whom?**
- *Possessions:* **Do you let others borrow your belongings?**

> If so, which ones? Who is able to borrow what, and for
> how long?
> - *Information:* What areas of your life are private? From
>   whom are they private? Under what circumstances and
>   with whom are you willing to share your most private
>   information?
> - *Personal space:* How close is too close?
> - *Time:* What do you say 'no' to?
> - *Emotions:* You are 'allowed' to feel the way you do, even if
>   others think you are being oversensitive or irrational.

You do not need to have the same boundary for everyone you interact with. For example, you may determine that you will only lend money to individuals within your nuclear family. Or you may share personal information about your relationships only with one or two people, while you freely tell people about your work or share your expertise.

I think it is worth thinking about the different people or groups who feature often in your life and work through each of these areas to determine what your boundaries are.

That said, in many ways, defining our boundaries is the easy part. How do we ensure that people do not invade our boundaries? How do we act in line with our boundaries? There is no easy solution to this. I think it takes practice at standing up for yourself and not feeling that you are being selfish, unfeeling, mean and so on. It is worth noting that if we do not uphold our boundaries in the moment when an issue first arises, we can assert ourselves later when we have had a chance to reflect. The objection I raised with my boss is an example of this (see page 19).

Defending our boundaries is an opportunity for us to employ our Three Companions; the compassion in this case can be directed towards ourselves as well as the persons concerned.

Self-care

The WHO definition of self-care is:

> The ability of individuals, families and communities to promote health, prevent disease, maintain health, and to cope with illness and disability with or without the support of a healthcare provider.[28]

This is a broad concept that covers a variety of areas, including health promotion, disease prevention and control, self-medication, providing care to dependent persons, seeking hospital or specialist care if necessary, and rehabilitation. This definition recognises that it is the individual person who acts to preserve health or respond to symptoms.

In the *Journal of Human Behaviour in the Social Environment*, Lisa D. Butler et al. state that self-care:

> requires consideration of the whole person and mindful attention and intentional efforts to achieve two general aims:
>
> 1. Guard against or manage stress and other negative states, and
> 2. Maintain or enhance well-being and overall functioning.[29]

In their paper, Butler and her co-authors examine what self-care looks like in six life domains: physical, professional, relational, emotional, psychological and spiritual. The intended audience is individuals working in the helping professions; however, I think there are lessons that we can all learn about effective self-care, so I would like to consider these in general terms next.

Physical self-care

This involves taking care of the body and ensuring an overall healthy lifestyle. This includes healthy eating, exercise, doing the things that you enjoy, getting enough sleep, being in nature and so forth. During the COVID-19 pandemic, we were encouraged to move and take frequent breaks. I was more cognisant of the variety of ways we can incorporate movement into our daily lives; for example, during phone meetings, walking coaching sessions, having a dance break to let our bodies move however they wanted, short strolls, gardening.

Professional self-care

This concerns taking care of ourselves in our place of work or study. It includes creating a workspace to our liking, taking time to chat with peers, managing our workload so that we take enough breaks, and developing outside interests, etc. I believe that professional self-care is being eroded as organisations and institutions continue to embrace remote working and learning environments.

In my work, I noticed that in the initial months of the pandemic there was extra pressure on individuals to juggle many things: running their households, taking care of and home-schooling their children, looking after elderly parents, performing at work, and taking care of themselves. People tended to be at their desks for longer hours due to increased workloads related to the pandemic (for example, disrupted supply chains, safe return to work, covering ill staff, lower employee engagement) without producing more outputs. Social connections were greatly reduced, with some informal video calls that waned over time. There was a blurring of physical boundaries between home and workspaces. I could see the toll that this was taking. This does not take account of the anxiety and fear that people felt about the pandemic and an uncertain future.

Relational self-care

This means being in a loving relationship with others. It is important to spend time with people we care about and to take time for ourselves. It is also about giving and receiving love, kindness and support, and getting rid of toxic relationships and healing old wounds. This has been hard during the lockdown restrictions imposed by governments to limit the spread of COVID-19. We have been grateful for the technology that has helped us to stay connected but we have missed the physical contact and simply being in the same space as other human beings. The pandemic has emphasised which people we want to remain close to and those relationships that no longer serve us and we want to ditch.

Emotional self-care

This involves being in a loving relationship with ourselves, and feeling our emotions without judgement. An important aspect of this relates to establishing our personal boundaries (discussed in the previous section). Other forms of emotional self-care include noticing our self-talk and challenging our inner critic, giving ourselves permission to take a break, addressing problems, enjoying hobbies, etc. This all relates to self-compassion.

Psychological self-care

This is about taking care of our minds: learning, thinking and growing. Activities in this realm might include taking time for personal reflection, noticing our inner thoughts, feelings and experiences, cultivating self-awareness, and engaging in personal and professional development. It is also about saying 'no' to taking on tasks or responsibilities when we do not have the capacity to do them without increasing our stress levels.

Spiritual self-care

This relates to connecting to purpose, meaning and essence. Principally, it is about knowing what is truly meaningful to us, what we stand and want to be remembered for, the non-material things in life, practising gratitude, prayer, meditation, religion and philosophy. The pandemic has given us the gift of slowing down. While we have lived under restrictions, we have had the chance to ponder our spiritual well-being and choose to re-set. In the CCW Community we have expressed a desire to retain some of the things we have learnt during our lockdowns. However, as the world re-opens, I can see that other forces make it difficult to make these shifts. For example, having benefited from not travelling for work, we may have chosen to reduce this aspect of our lives, only to wrestle with the competing demands of employers, clients and colleagues.

Daily self-care

Self-care is idiosyncratic. There is no 'one size fits all' plan that works for everyone. If we are giving a lot of ourselves to others, we need to take time to rest, reflect, replenish and renew ourselves. If we don't, we are in danger of becoming stressed, burnt out and experiencing compassion fatigue. We can only sustain what we are giving to others with what we are giving to ourselves.

Some ways we can do this include:

- Practices that still the mind; for example, meditation, yoga, journaling.
- Activities that we enjoy, such as gardening, cooking, reading, listening to music, playing an instrument, dancing, poetry, luxuriating in a bath, having a massage; anything that transports us mentally to a different place.
- Podcasts, which I personally find can give me new ideas about how I view life. I particularly enjoy listening to interviews of individuals who have something to say about one or all Three Companions, such as Krista Tippett (On Being),[30] Dan Harris (Ten Percent Happier),[31] Joshua Steindfeldt (The Courageous Life),[32] Brené Brown[33] and Elizabeth Gilbert,[34] to name a few.

Self-care was touched on by some of my interviewees. For example, Idris (see page 62) was very aware of his natural response to stress: 'When I'm under stress, I close up. I become the opposite of what needs to happen, which is to communicate and talk to people.'

In addition to enabling us to reveal our Three Companions, self-care has other benefits, including:

- Better physical health
- Improved resistance to disease
- Better productivity
- Enhanced self-esteem
- Increased self-knowledge
- More to give others[35]

Well worth the investment, don't you think?

Support network

In many of the stories, my interviewees were able to draw on the help of others to support them. As we now know, to bring compassion into the world takes a lot of courage and wisdom to enable us to do that in the right way. Having people with whom we can talk through our struggles and concerns was extremely valuable for many of those I spoke to. This came in a variety of guises, including counsellors, therapists, peers, colleagues, mentors, coaches, family, friends and partners.

The support we receive from others can take the form of a small action – for example, words of theirs that challenge our mindset – or it can be a significant intervention such as therapy. The fact that these people are there for and with us, in either a professional or personal capacity, can help us to exercise our Three Companions in our dealings with ourselves and others.

We can be intentional about getting the support we need by cultivating a network of individuals who we can turn to in our time of need. It is worth investing some time to think through who we have around us and how they help or hinder us through their support, or lack of it. Some questions you can ask are:

- What is it that they do that I find helpful?
- What don't I appreciate?
- Who is missing from the individuals I normally turn to? Why?
- What can I do to ensure that I get the help I need at the right time?

When we analyse our network, we can identify whether there are gaps and/or individuals who are not providing the support we need from them. This gives us the opportunity to redress this if we choose.

I rely heavily on my own support network to help me through taxing times. When I was going through an extremely fraught time with my husband, I worked with an addiction prevention specialist to help me cope. She invited me to scrutinise my support network. I put people's names into different categories: family, friends, professional/medical. Then I examined what support I was receiving from each person, what I found helpful and any actions that were problematic to me. I realised that I was disappointed in one person who claimed to be there for me but only was when I asked. He was not proactive in his support. I called him to ask about it and we cleared the air. We realised that there were misunderstandings on both sides.

I also realised that my father was not in my support network. When I assessed this, it was because I feared that I would receive his judgement rather than his compassion. It took some courage for me to contact him and let him know what was happening in my life. He did mete out the advice that I expected, and I was prepared for it. I was glad that I had included him specifically because it also prepared my father a little for my husband's death.

The CCW Community has similarly become a support network for the people who participate in it. I have been amazed at how it has grown from tentative beginnings to a place where individuals feel supported, either through active participation in the discussions, or from the weekly emails that I send out with my reflections on the topics and discussions that have arisen that week. The bonds that have formed amongst strangers over the course of a year are stronger than I could ever have imagined. We hold each other in a safe space of caring that is magical.

Identifying our support network can be a painful exercise if we have lost loved ones. We need to be mindful of our grief and be gentle and kind to ourselves. When we are ready, we can identify who can help us to rebuild the support and care that we need and have lost with the passing of those special individuals who were there for us in the past.

Continuing on

I would like to sustain my research into how and when we employ our Three Companions and how the five domains sketched in this chapter support or hinder that. What nuances do we need to deepen our relationship with our Three Companions? Some avenues I would like to explore are:

- How do our Three Companions evolve over time?
- What are the characteristics of individuals who more readily reveal their Three Companions?
- What do these three virtues look like in different parts of the world?

This feels like a worthwhile pursuit that accords with my life purpose.

In closing...

We have come to the end of this undertaking. In the beginning, I stated why I wanted to write this book: to help people see themselves in the stories of others and gain confidence in their own abilities to exercise their Three Companions. *Why bother?* you might ask yourself. Why put all this effort into revealing our Three Companions? What are the benefits of operating from the intersection of courage, compassion, and wisdom?

I believe the stories that you have read in these pages illustrate that we can have a profound, positive impact on others, and ourselves, when we are able to act from the triple helix that is courage, compassion and wisdom. The interplay of the Three Companions is synergistic; they are greater together than the sum of the individual parts. They enable us to face into demanding situations in a humanistic way that puts people at the heart of what we are striving for. On occasion, that person is us; we deserve to be shown the same courage, compassion, and wisdom as everybody else. With our Three Companions, we can deeply listen to ourselves and others and respond appropriately to alleviate suffering and effect change. Note this is not always by acting: sometimes doing nothing is the most courageous, compassionate and wisest act.

I strongly believe that courage allows us to bring compassion into the world, to be alongside suffering. Slowing down allows us to get in tune with the wisdom that is available to us – both our own and the collective wisdom in the world. Milly told me that one thing she had learnt is that she needs time: 'I find that taking two steps back, *insisting* on time to consider, is crucial to making the right decision in a difficult situation, particularly one that involves any kind of conflict. Remembering to take that time is something that's very hard to achieve, but at least I now know that that's what I need!' In so doing, we can all affect profound change, one person at a time.

The people I spoke with identified the positive impact of the Three Companions at three levels:

1. *Individual*: Giving rise to increased self-belief, confidence and personal growth.
2. *Our communities*: These include family, friend circles, neighbourhoods and organisations. We are able to connect in a different way with members of our communities. We are more open, honest, non-judgemental, supportive and caring. We create space for others to be themselves. As a result, we are more inclusive, kinder to each other, relieve suffering, have an increased chance of success in our work and deliver better outcomes.
3. *World*: Our actions enable us to tackle issues that have global impact; for example, climate change, mental health, discrimination and inclusion.

Let them tell you in their own words…

Individual level

'The benefit is to us because we grow, we learn more. You're more open. You realise that you're a human being, and we are here for one another. If you're able to give, you grow more, and you're at peace with yourself. You have more harmony within yourself. You can see why people behave the way they do. You're more discerning of people who hurt you or you can find the reason for it. When you can find the reason, you're not vindictive.'

Community level

'I think the organisation can achieve better things, because they create a better environment in which people can thrive. And if you look at it from that wider perspective and different lenses, then you've got to feel safer, haven't you, if you can do all of those three?'

'I suppose every tiny, good thing you put into the world helps it develop better. Other people will see you and learn from you. You might learn from somebody else's compassionate, wise or courageous act. You say, "Very brave", or, "That's very correct." Or, "That's nice. I'd like to be a little more like that." Even if you do it subconsciously, I think it rubs off and it spreads.'

World level

'I was thinking: courage, compassion and wisdom are connected as a system. And I think about how our world systems are getting out of balance. So, we've become a self-serving culture, particularly in the Western world. Our ecosystems and those types of systems are starting to get out of balance. I'm a strong believer that this horrendous situation we find ourselves in is the system giving us a warning that something has to shift. I think that as a system within a system, wisdom, courage, and compassion is one of the ways that we can lean into, to help ourselves and others around us to make some of those shifts.'

'I do believe it makes the world a better place. What I mean is that we are social beings as humans. We function more effectively in a world where we can hold in balance those Three Companions and we can rely on them at different points in time and to different degrees and strengths.'

I have immensely enjoyed writing this book. I feel honoured that my interviewees trusted me to tell their stories in a way that dignified them, so that we can learn and grow in our expression of courage, compassion and wisdom. I feel passionately that the Three Companions permit us to perform magic in our environment and transform lives.

Courage, Compassion, and Wisdom
Are three values, three virtues,
Three Companions,
That climb up around each other,
Having fun,
Rising higher and higher,
Till we look back and recognise how far we've come.

Thank you for coming on this journey with me.

Notes

Introduction

[1] Employee resource groups (ERGs) are voluntary employee-led groups that build community, provide support, contribute to personal and professional development, and advocate for their members. Their aim is to promote diverse and inclusive workplaces. While their membership is predominantly formed by individuals with shared identities and experiences, individuals who want to support these groups and who have different identities are also welcome. Examples of these groups are: women, people of colour, neurodiverse, early career, LGBTQ+. These groups are consulted more and more often to inform organisational strategy, so that the term increasingly used to describe them is 'business resource groups' (BRGs). Other terms in use include 'affinity groups'. See: www.greatplacetowork.com/resources/blog/what-are-employee-resource-groups-ergs and www.catalyst.org/topics/ergs/ https://medium.com/sarah-cordivano/employee-resource-groups-part-1-b684aa249420

[2] See: www.huffpost.com/entry/azim-khamisa-and-ples-felix_n_5c632ab1e4b03de942966727

[3] See: www.ted.com/talks/azim_khamisa_and_ples_felix_what_comes_after_tragedy_forgiveness/transcript?language=en

[4] 'Brexit' and 'Brin' are the terms coined to encapsulate the options in the UK referendum to leave the European Union and remain. The outcome of the vote in 2016 was to leave.

Part One

[5] See: www.linkedin.com/pulse/flourish-five-practices-particularly-resilient-people-taryn/

[6] See: www.linkedin.com/pulse/fearless-taryn-stejskal-ph-d-/

[7] David Whyte, *Consolations: the Solace, Nourishment and Underlying Meaning of Everyday Words* (Edinburgh: Canongate Books Limited, 2014), p. 32.

[8] Pema Chödrön, *When Things Fall Apart; Heart Advice for Difficult Times* (London: Element, 2005), pp. 103–11.

[9] See: https://en.wikipedia.org/wiki/Triple_helix_model_of_innovation

Part Two

[10] Dr Taryn Marie Stejskal (see: www.resilience-leadership.com/our-story) has identified the five practices of particularly resilient people; see: www.resilience-leadership.com/resilience-blog/five-practices-of-particularly-resilient-people. One of these is a term that she coins as 'grati-osity', which is a combination of gratitude and generosity.

[11] Chris Germer, 'A Comprehensive Overview of Self-Compassion', talk at the Compassion in Therapy Summit, 2021, www.compassionintherapy.com/stream/chris-germer-2/

[12] The change curve is a theory that was developed by Elisabeth Kübler-Ross to describe how people react to change. There are several stages that individuals go through. These are shock, denial, frustration, depression, experiment, decision and integration. It is not a linear process and individuals may oscillate between stages before moving to acceptance. The key is to recognise and help people move through the change curve. The key is to recognise and help people move through the change curve. See: www.ekrfoundation.org/5-stages-of-grief/change-curve/

[13] There are several versions of this prayer. This seems to be one of the earliest versions.

[14] MCO – Movement Control Order; due to COVID-19.

[15] The amygdala is part of the limbic system in the brain that is involved in perceiving, learning and regulating emotions. It detects all emotions and processes them in order of importance. Fear is the most significant. You have probably heard of the flight, fight, freeze response to perceived danger; the amygdala is responsible for that.

[16] 'Page 3' became a colloquialism in the UK for photos of topless women in tabloid newspapers. This was popularised by the *Sun* newspaper.

Part Three

[17] See: www.pexels.com

[18] See: https://unsplash.com

[19] See: https://hbr.org/2020/11/self-compassion-will-make-you-a-better-leader

[20] See: https://self-compassion.org/about

[21] See: https://self-compassion.org/wp-content/uploads/publications/Mindfulness_and_SC_chapter_in_press.pdf

[22] Kristin Neff's website provides some ideas and resources that will help you to develop your self-compassion practice. See: https://self-compassion.org

[23] See: www.compassioninstitute.com/the-program/compassion-education-training

[24] Dr Kristin Neff, 'The Power of Self-Compassion', talk at the Compassion in Therapy Summit, 2021. See: www.compassionintherapy.com

[25] Chris Germer, 'A Comprehensive Overview of Self-Compassion', talk at the Compassion in Therapy Summit, 2021. See: www.compassionintherapy.com

[26] Chris Germer writes about fierce compassion and what it is not in this article: https://centerformsc.org/the-near-enemies-of-fierce-compassion/

[27] www.psychologytoday.com/us/blog/constructive-wallowing/201604/3-essential-ways-protect-your-personal-boundaries

[28] See: www.who.int/reproductivehealth/self-care-interventions/definitions/en/

[29] Lisa D. Butler, Kelly A. Mercer et al., 'Six Domains of Self-care: Attending to the Whole Person', *Journal of Human Behaviour in the Social Environment* (2019) 29:1, pp. 107–124.

[30] See: https://onbeing.org/series/podcast

[31] See: www.tenpercent.com/podcast

[32] See: https://joshuasteinfeldt.com

[33] See: https://brenebrown.com

[34] See: www.elizabethgilbert.com/bio

[35] See: www.thelawofattraction.com/self-care-tips

Acknowledgements

With thanks to:

My mother, Blossom, for the strength and courage that you have shown throughout your life that has enabled me to find my own path.

Bertie and Emily, my son and daughter, who have become wonderful adults who inspire and encourage me in their individual ways. Without you, Bertie, there would have been no book. Emily, you are my no. 1 cheerleader; your belief in me and enthusiasm are infectious.

Lizzie and Stephen, who have given me the priceless gift of their presence, particularly through turbulent times. You have each provided me with a safe space to shelter when the going was tough and accepted me without judgement. For that, I am truly grateful.

Tara, for your generosity of spirit and conviction in the Three Companions and our work together. And lovely Gusta, whose diffidence gave me the idea for the book.

Jane, the development editor who worked with me on the book. You showed me how to transform my text into a manuscript in a way that was motivating and energising.

Michelle, who bravely challenged herself and channelled her Three Companions to design this beautiful book cover.

The individuals whose thoughts and stories about the Three Companions feature in this book. Your response to my enquiry was mind-blowing. The more I talked with you, the more confidence I gained in my endeavour. Thank you for your generosity which will enable others to learn and grow.

About the author

Joan van den Brink is a leading executive coach who works internationally with senior business leaders and managers. After graduating from the University of Cambridge with a PhD in Chemistry, she embarked on a career in marketing and moved from there into operations management. She went on to become a management consultant whose fields of expertise include talent management, leadership development and individual and team coaching. She then joined a speciality chemicals company as Executive Vice President HR & Communications, where she led the development of both functions. In 2014, she set up her own consultancy, working with clients on a range of strategic topics and issues to enable their people to be the best they can be. Today, she focuses on supporting organisations and individuals to create inclusive environments in which diverse people can thrive.